CREATE YOUR

Carl-Johan
Forssén Ehrlin

FUTURE

Discover The Power of the Mind and
Learn How to Take Full Control of Your Life!

Translation by Karin Shearman

e.

EHRLIN PUBLISHING

OTHER BOOKS BY CARL-JOHAN FORSSÉN EHRLIN

The Tractor Who Wants to Fall Asleep (Ehrlin Publishing, 2017)
The Elephant Who Wants to Fall Asleep (Penguin Random House, 2016)
The Rabbit Who Wants to Fall Asleep (Penguin Random House, 2015)

Originally published in Sweden by Ehrlin Publishing © 2017
Original title: Skapa din framtid – En handbok i ledarskap och personlig utveckling
© 2019 Carl-Johan Forssén Ehrlin and Ehrlin Publishing AB

Translation to English © 2019 Karin Shearman
Cover and design: Elin Westerberg
Cover photo: Jonas Nygren

ISBN: 978-91-88375-33-9
www.ehrlinpublishing.com
www.carl-johan.com

CONTENTS

FOREWORD TO THE NEW EDITION

In 2006, the first edition of this book was released. During this period of my life I studied psychology and pedagogy along with other interesting topics related to people and how we think and act. I listened actively to audio books about personal development and attended courses where I explored myself from the inside and out, aiming to get to know myself a bit better. I had also just started my first company which was aimed at helping individuals and managers to develop and feel good about themselves.

In parallel with my studies and my business, I was heavily involved in the Swedish Armed Forces as a volunteer Officer. All the lessons I learned from studying theories and then applying them to reality became the foundation of *Create Your Future – A Guide to Leadership and Personal Development*, and then my success as a writer of books, sold globally in their millions, began.

Success can take many forms. For me, it has always been to be able to contribute to a better world. A world where people feel good, sleep well and are happy. What has largely led to my success as a writer and entrepreneur is that I have practiced what I have learned. Although the book was originally written several years ago, the experiences I have written about are truly what have created my future and allowed me to follow my mission and passion to help people, now on an even wider scale.

Jönköping, Sweden, 2017
Carl-Johan Forssén Ehrlin

FOREWORD

As I see it, life is more enjoyable and fulfilling if you come to some insights. These insights often centre around your perceptions of other people, but sometimes the most important insights are in how you perceive yourself – the only person you truly have the power to change.

My own journey into self-development is best described as going from night to day. I gained a whole new way of looking at life and I now want to share my insights with you. My hope is that this book will help you to grow and learn more about yourself and your surroundings.

It is also a book about leadership, suitable for both those with an identifiable leadership role as a manager, group leader or parent, and for those who play an everyday role in a group, family or team and wish to understand better the dynamics of the group. The book is aimed at those who are both new to the idea as well as those who have already begun their journey towards personal development and leadership. There are chapters to suit everyone and you should use them exactly as you please. For simplicity, I mainly use the term "he" in the examples but, of course, all examples and types of personality apply equally well to women.

I have strived to be as straightforward as possible to make for simple reading and to enable you to easily apply the tips in the book directly in your own life. However, it is important that you do not simply accept everything I have written. Read, analyse and test to see if it is right for you too. Test my advice fully before you accept or reject it.

Create Your Future is carefully planned with a common thread throughout the book, where you are gradually introduced to the building blocks to build upon previous chapters. The book begins with chapters on personal development and personal leadership, to enable us to lead others. If we strive to become successful as leaders, development must begin within ourselves.

Feel free to take breaks for reflection between reading the different chapters as you progress through the book. I want to emphasise that the book is not simply meant to be read from cover to cover, but may also be used as a reference book since the different chapters are almost independent of one another. But, in my view, all chapters are connected and form a whole that will enhance your understanding of the outside world and yourself as a person, so you should read the entire book at least once. If you feel that you need to repeat a certain topic, you can return to that chapter rather than read the whole book again.

Nothing makes me special. I am just a normal person who decided to write a book and live my life based upon its principles. Keep in mind as you read the book that this is my interpretation of the world, but it may just change your own view of life too. My aim with the book is to encourage you to open your mind and look with new eyes upon yourself and on life. As you use my tips and thoughts in your own life, you will most likely notice some immediate results and discover that you are developing yourself even further. I hope you will enjoy my book!

Huskvarna, Sweden, 2006
Carl-Johan Forssén Ehrlin

CHAPTER 1
THE POWER OF THOUGHT

MENTAL BOUNDARIES

One of the main weaknesses of mankind is the average man's familiarity with the word "impossible." He knows all the rules which will not work. He knows all the things which cannot be done.
– Napoleon Hill

Did you know that circus elephants, tied up by only a thin rope, never run away? They could very much do so if they wished. The reason that they don't run away is that, from a very early age, they have been trained to believe they cannot. From the outset, their keepers used heavy chains or ropes which could not be shifted when the elephants pulled at them. In adulthood, the chains and heavy ropes were replaced by thinner ones which were easier for the keepers to handle. Through their previous experiences, the elephants were convinced that it was impossible to break the chains.

Just like the circus elephants, people can be tied to a thought pattern that they think is the only right one, and sometimes it is hard to break the pattern. Most of us have been conditioned to believe in one or more mental "ropes" which confine us, for example: "you'll never amount to anything" or "hard work is the only way to earn money in life". What parallels can you draw between the elephant and your own life? Do you have ropes from your childhood which hold you back and prevent you from growing and being the person you want to be?

Most of the ropes we grow up with are not real – they are created by society or the people around us. In most cases we do not know who created these mental constraints as they are often developed unconsciously over an extended period of time.

To illustrate the idea of mental constraints, I will use an exercise taken from Bo Ahrenfelt's book *Förändring som tillstånd* (*Change as a State of Mind*, translators note). I urge you to carry out the exercise to understand the power of what Bo Ahrenfelt calls "the prison of thought". Use the example in the book or draw the dots on a piece of paper.

» Draw four straight lines without lifting the pen from the paper.

» The lines must all go through all of the points.

» You may never pass the same point twice.

Did you find it easy? Now try to do the same exercise using only three lines. If you are feeling especially confident, try with only one line. Is it even possible.

Compare your efforts with the solutions on the next page, but solve it yourself first – there are no shortcuts to insights in life!

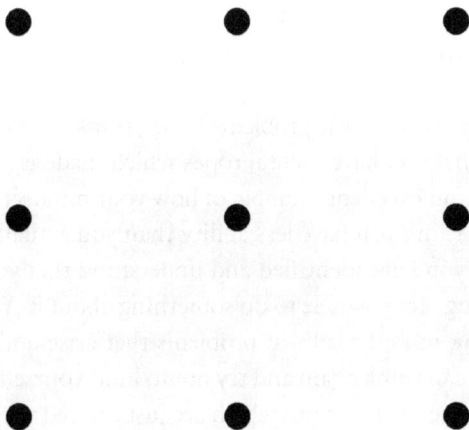

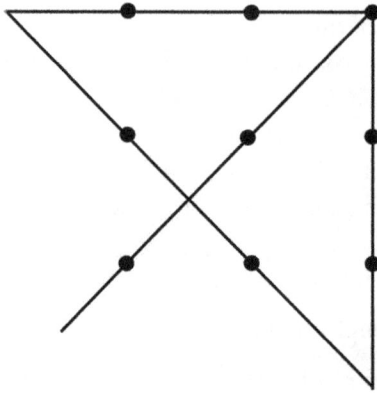

Solution with four lines.

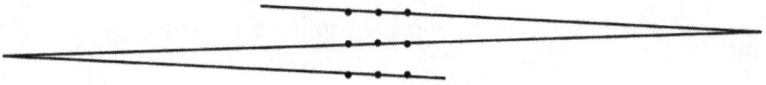

Solution with three lines.

Did you manage to solve the problem? If not, think a little why not. Did you discover that you have mental ropes which made it more difficult? This exercise is an excellent example of how your mindset can limit you and make you think you have less ability than you actually do.

Only when you have identified and understood that you are limited in your thinking, are you able to do something about it. You can decide to start looking more broadly at problems that arise and find suitable solutions. You can think again and try not to limit yourself to the conditions you perceive are there but which are just created within your own mind or by society.

FIRST AND SECOND ORDER THOUGHT

There are many different ways of looking at a problem and finding a solution. According to Bo Ahrenfelt, you can either use the first or the second order thought. If you, when trying to solve the problem of the prison of thought, told yourself or those around you: "It doesn't work" or "I need an extra line, otherwise it's not possible!" or "if I take away the dot in the middle, it'll work" – then you've tried to solve the problem using first order thought. This way of solving problems is characterised by the mindset: "We can't run the business like this anymore, we must file for bankruptcy" or "we need to downsize one of our departments if we are to continue". Privately, it can be about your inner dreams – you assume that they cannot be reached for a variety of reasons. Solving a problem by adding or removing the same kind of resources, you remain in the same mindset as you were before and will likely achieve comparable results.

In the second order thought, the problem no longer lies in the problem itself, but in how we handle it. Ahrenfelt also believes that we have become used to using first order problem-solving. We can no longer rely on first order solutions but must begin to question our own problem solving and find fresh solutions outside the box. This means we move away from an "adding or removing resources" mentality and begin to question ourselves and our own systems for finding a solution. A company which is doing badly will ask itself: "How can we develop to become successful again?". A person with dreams of changing his life in different ways, will ask himself: What do I need to do, learn or think differently if I am to achieve my goals and dreams?

When you shift from first to the second order thought, you begin to question yourself rather than the problem. This will probably mean that you'll encounter some resistance within yourself and those around you. This resistance must be overcome, and as you solve the problem, it will lead to personal development within yourself. If your immediate boss has an authoritative leadership style when it comes to problem solving, it may result in you never reaching the second order thought. If your boss already thinks he knows what is best and is bound by the first order thought, he or she is unlikely to be open to innovative ways of solving the problem. As soon as you let go of your preconceptions of how things and people should be, you open yourself up to the second order thought and become susceptible to make larger-scale changes.

If you broaden your thinking, you can solve the problem of the prison of thought with a single line by drawing it around the globe. Was that the first solution you thought of?

A FICTIONAL REALITY

There is a whole science dedicated to how society creates values and norms for what can and cannot be created, what can and cannot be done, what researchers say is and is not possible. It is called *social constructivism*, and theories of this science challenge our thinking of why things are as they are. Why a chair is called a chair instead of, for example, a brick. This way of thinking can raise huge questions and it is easy to start questioning the whole society why things are the way they are.

A good example of social constructivism is the story about the moment when a human being first ran an English mile in under four minutes.

Throughout the ages, scientists had said that the human body was not made to run that fast, that our muscles could not handle it. Even the ancient Greeks are said to have tied people behind horses in an attempt to beat this invisible time barrier, but without success. Until 1954, it was said that it was impossible for man to run an English mile (approximately 1,600 metres) in under four minutes. But one man, Roger Bannister, did not believe it to be impossible. Roger Bannister was a student of medicine, which put restrictions on the time he had available to train for his running. However, he was determined that he could beat the magical four-minute barrier. He gradually trained and conditioned himself, competed and progressed towards his goal. Then, on 6th May 1954, the breakthrough came – he ran a mile in under four minutes, a feat which scientists and the general public thought impossible. After Roger Bannister's success, the four-minute barrier was beaten by someone else just 54 days later, and by several other people after that.

What was it that made us unable to run that fast sooner? The answer is that it was generally accepted that we were not designed to cope with running at such speed. Thanks to the will and passion of one person to defeat the invisible time limit, we discovered that, not only could we do it, but we could run even faster still. Today, the world record for running a mile has become even faster and currently sits at 3:43:13. The record is held by the Moroccan Hicham El Guerrouj.

What other mental barriers do you think exist in our society and within yourself? Have you begun to realise that they need not be barriers to you? Instead they can be seen as challenges which you can overcome if you train and prepare yourself, both mentally and physically.

CHALLENGE YOUR COMFORT ZONE

A comfort zone is a state of mind or a situation where you feel safe and secure. Being in your comfort zone means that you avoid exposing yourself to things which feel uncomfortable, difficult or unpleasant. Instead, you choose the comfortable and safe option when confronting different situations.

The American lecturer, Bob Harrison, once drew a parallel between a person's comfort zone and the invisible fence used to keep dogs within a given area, such as a garden. The fence is designed using sound waves which only dogs can hear. The sound emitted is unpleasant for the dog and they are reluctant to pass through it, so they retire as soon as they approach. They would rather remain within the confines of the garden than withstand the discomfort of the sound trap. Do you recognise yourself? Do you remain within an invisible fence in order to avoid the pain and demands that are always experienced when you are developing?

There is an old saying: "No pain, no gain". How many situations have you found yourself in where you chose to sit in the background or fail to fulfil your true potential just because it may be embarrassing, difficult or affect other people? I am certain that, on occasions, you have chosen the comfortable road instead of the more challenging or difficult one. We all do it sometimes.

To clarify my thoughts about comfort zones, I would like to tell you about a man called Ted. Ted is 52 years old and lives in a house in a small village. He has lived alone in the same place since he first moved away from his parents at the age of 20. He works in a nearby factory and has had the same job since he began as a young 19-year-old. Every day, he knows exactly what he will be doing at work. He has had the same responsibilities at work for 33 years and his company is still making the same products as when Ted first started there. When computers were introduced to the workplace, Ted complained to his management and didn't understand at all what use they would be. Ted didn't like the change.

Ted has a cat which he always feeds as soon as he comes home from work. He then sits in front of the television and watches the same series and news programmes every day. He used to use his cat as an excuse for not going out and taking part in social activities with his colleagues. He would much rather sit at home and watch television. Now his colleagues don't invite him anymore. Because of that, Ted has never met anyone to share his life with.

Many people can identify themselves with Ted and his situation. Can you?

What if Ted were confronted with a number of changes. How do you think he would cope with the following examples?

» The company's management has decided to invest in a new product and will shut down the old production completely. Ted will be reassigned to a new role. They will also introduce a new three-shift system which will sometimes require him to work evenings and nights.

» For a long time, Ted has wondered what it would be like to fall in love and share his life with somebody. One day, a nice woman named Maria begins working at Ted's company. She shows some interest in Ted and insists that they meet up. Ted, shyly and somewhat reluctantly, agrees to meet outside of work and to go for a walk together. They fall in love and, after a while, Maria wants to move into a new place together.

» The company's investment in the new product did not go well and they have had to dismiss Ted. He is now facing an uncertain future.

» The car Ted uses to get to and from work is an old Amazon which he was given by his parents on his 20th birthday, just before they died. Now the car is old and faulty and needs to be changed.

» Ted wins on a lottery scratch card and now must appear on television for the chance to win the jackpot.

For many people, these types of situations are not uncommon and are relatively easy to deal with. But if you have lived behind an invisible fence, such did the dogs in the previous example, such changes can be overwhelming.

Do you think any of the situations are negative for Ted? What can you learn from these examples? As a leader, can you identify such challenges amongst your employees?

A MENTAL MAP WHICH INFLUENCES OUR CHOICES

There is a branch within personal development that stems from psychology, called Neuro Linguistic Programming (NLP). It was developed by two Americans, Richard Bandler and John Grinder, in the early 1970s. NLP is primarily concerned with communication, within ourselves and with others. It is also concerned with how you can use speech and communication to influence yourself and others to create positive change.

Within NLP is the theory that we are guided by mental maps throughout our lives. We all carry a mental "backpack" with different values, beliefs, behaviours and strategies which we use for solving problems. It is the contents of your backpack which shape your mental map and influence your decisions and ultimately what you achieve in life. If you were brought up with negative beliefs, they will influence all your achievements, whether you are aware of it or not.

To show what I mean, I want you to visualise the following situation for a moment:

» A man stood at a crossroads.

What did the man look like? Was he wearing a jacket? A hat? Was he happy or sad? What was the crossroads like? Was it busy or deserted? What time of year was it? Which way did he go after he'd stood at the crossroads?

If you carry out this exercise with your friends and compare the results, you will discover something very exciting: everyone thinks differently. There is no exact copy of the mental map you carry around. Everyone sees different crossroads; no other crossroads looked exactly like the one you thought of. No-one has experienced the exact same things you have nor drawn the same lessons as you have. A lesson from mental maps is that we all think differently due to our earlier experiences. If your map did not lead you to a goal you wanted to reach, you must begin to change your map to get closer to the goal. To be successful in what you aim for, you need to work on your mental map and expand it, see and think differently and therefore achieve new results.

A subconscious observation from my childhood was that women always did everything in the kitchen. My mother was a housewife and I grew up with the view that women do everything around the home. I took this observation with me for a while after I moved in with the woman in my life, which became the cause of many conflicts in our relationship without us ever really knowing why. The problem with observations, is that we often act unconsciously because of them, without ever stopping first to reflect. Observations create behaviours that occur automatically.

It is only when you stop and question your own actions that you can make a change. In my case, it hit me one day why I was so reluctant to help out in the kitchen, and it was only once I'd realised the reason for my behaviour that I could begin to change it. Nowadays, my values have changed and one of the most enjoyable things my wife and I do together is cook in the kitchen and talk about life.

CONTROL YOUR THOUGHTS

Another idea within NLP is that you, as an individual, have a real ability to influence how you react to different situations. To learn how to control your reactions, it is important to reflect on what has taken place, as soon as it has happened. The next step is to determine how you will react in a similar situation while it is happening. Practice on how you identify, think and act in different situations. Once you become used to an automatic response, you can make an active choice about how you react to it next time. By training yourself to reflect and act as you *want* to act, you will develop better self-control and avoid many conflicts and negative behaviours which are all-to-often unnecessary.

Have you ever been really irritated by something and, all of a sudden, something unexpected happened which has caused you to completely forget your irritation and calm down? In some areas of psychology, it is said that people are guided by different so-called thought patterns in different situations. If something unexpected happens which is not included as part of the routine, your brain loses track of it and your reaction or behaviour changes. The ability to break or disrupt a routine can be used consciously to give a positive result. For example, my wife and I have been practicing to use this technique and we find it very useful.

The next time someone in your family or one of your friends becomes irritated at you without any real reason, try to break the pattern by doing something completely unexpected. Jump up and down on one leg, or do something else funny or unexpected. You will immediately notice a mood shift towards a happier behaviour. We made this a habit in our house; when one of us became irritated by some small trifle, the other did something funny which made the sourpuss lose track of the irritation and return to a more positive frame of mind. But it is important to agree these rules in advance when all parties are feeling well-balanced. If you skip this part and just try to break the thought pattern when someone is firmly irritated, you can just make the situation worse.

You can use the same technique on yourself. If you find yourself angry or ill-tempered, you can start laughing to yourself or think about something crazy or weird. You'll quickly lose your irritation and begin thinking in new ways again.

VISUALISE

A well-known concept nowadays is to *visualise*. But what does it really mean? Why should we do it? Well, visualising means that you see yourself doing something which has not yet happened. In your mind, you imagine how a certain situation will pan out. You decide in advance how you will react and therefore broaden your thinking. You could say that you consciously create the thought path that you want the brain to follow when it comes to it. By mentally preparing for what is to come, you will not feel the same worry, nervousness or other negative feelings that you would usually experience in that situation. Because you have already rehearsed the situation with a positive outcome in mind, it is easier to achieve the same result in reality.

Imagine that you have set a goal of running a certain distance in a certain time. Just before you go out and run, sit down and visualise. See in your mind that you are running and sense just how light and easy it feels today. You see yourself running the whole distance and finishing well within the time you have set yourself. You don't feel at all exhausted and have energy to spare. Do the exercise with as much enthusiasm as possible to reach the best possible result.

What happens is that you trick your subconscious into thinking that you can actually run that fast. Because you believe it, you improve your chances of achieving it. Actually achieving your target time depends upon how realistic you have been based upon your current physical condition but, even if you don't manage it, you'll notice a marked difference when you run. You will find that you'll run a little faster than you normally do.

If you begin to lose your pace as you run, simply repeat the visualisation exercise to yourself so that you pick it up again. Each time I have stopped improving in my training, I use the visualisation technique on myself. I see myself reaching the next goal – and I usually achieve it.

CHAPTER 2
POSITIVE AND INQUISITIVE ATTITUDE

Did you know that many people in Tibet begin each morning giving thanks for their lives reaching a new day and that in the evening they give thanks for the day that has just been? Are you also thankful for the fact that you are here and that you have woken to the chance of a new and wonderful day? Or are you, like many others, someone who thinks life is at its worst when you first open your eyes in the morning? If you relate to the latter, maybe you should take a look at your life and try to find something which makes you happy and motivates you to hop out of bed as soon as you wake up.

Let me set you a challenge: For a whole week, wake up every morning and concentrate your mind into thinking that life is beautiful. Do your best to really believe it. At the end of the week, evaluate the exercise – did you experience any differences? Did your days turn out better?

INQUISITIVE LEARNING

Have a little think about which members of our society learn the most.

I believe it is children around 6-years old. Small children are curious and ask lots of questions. They want to know how everything works. Do you recognise that? Do you have your own children or have you met children around that age? They are always asking: "Why? Why? Why?". You also notice, when you interact with these children, that they are quick to learn and will even begin to correct us adults when we do or say something wrong.

How can we, as adults, learn anything from such children? Well, we

can begin by doing exactly as they do and posing the question: "Why?".
Why did that happen or why does it work that way? When you are working
on your own personal development, a curious and inquisitive attitude
is useful to start challenging your old way of thinking and acting. In
case of failure, take a moment to step back and ask yourself what you
can learn from that situation. What were the positives amongst all the
failures? Why did it go as it did? How can I prevent it from happening
again?

I was once at a university graduation ceremony. On the podium
stood the university's Vice-Principal. He proclaimed how much more
wonderful the world would be if we asked the question: "Why?". He
suggested that all science is based upon asking why. He continued that,
long ago, man saw the skies merely as a dome, dotted with white spots.
Today we know that there is a whole universe out there and that the
white spots are stars, just like our own sun, and there is no known end
to this universe. The question: "Why?" leads to many new insights.

Be generous with asking "Why?", so you get a greater understanding
of the world and the people in it. This will lead to a new and beautiful
view of people and your environment, just like the stars on a clear night.

THE SEVEN QUESTIONS TECHNIQUE

By keeping an open mind, try not to be locked into your old thought
patterns. There is an Asian technique for highlighting problems by looking at them from new perspectives. This is called the seven questions
technique, where you ask "Why?" at least seven times in a row, which
reminds us of the young inquisitive child.

The technique goes like this. Present your problem to a partner, for
example: "It is so cold in our house". Your partner has a simple job to
do, he or she may simply just say: "Why?" in different ways. In this case,
your partner replies with "Why is that?". You may answer: "Because
we have bad insulation": The partner then asks: "Why do you have bad
insulation?". "Because we decided to install the insulation ourselves".
"Why did you decide to do it yourselves?". And so on. I have both used

and been on the receiving end of this technique when there has been someone or something I didn't understand. Each time it has led to a deeper understanding of the nature of the problem, as opposed to just the "symptom" (in this case that the house was cold).

ALWAYS HAVE FUN

Is it possible to always have fun? I am convinced that it is. It does not mean that you should avoid those things you find boring, rather that you should alter your perspective of it and do your best to make it enjoyable.

One example of how you can make a boring activity fun, is how I think before having to clean the bathroom at home. I usually give myself a challenge. Something like: "I am expecting guests in three minutes and have to hurry to clean the bathroom before they arrive". What motivates me is achieving something in a way that hasn't been done before, or achieving something under some sort of time pressure. If someone says to me that nobody has ever cleaned a bathroom in under three minutes, I will do everything within my power to do it faster. I would find the cleaning task fun, whether I achieved my three-minute goal or not. In my case, it always works when I set myself challenges, but you might have to do it in some other way. Can you come up with some way of making mundane or boring things enjoyable?

I learned this technique when I was employed by a manpower agency and assigned to various monotonous jobs within industry. It was around the same period that I began training myself in personal development. As I worked, I listened to audio books about having the right attitude, and this awoke ideas about making my work more enjoyable. How could I make a monotonous task fun? I began trying what I'd learned from the books; to always have a positive outlook towards life and the challenges I faced. Every day, I set challenges for myself, for example that I should produce X number of products, that I would chat to X number of people, that I should have a better relationship with my boss, and so on. All of a sudden, the work became much more fun.

People are motivated in different ways. Find out what motivates you and use that in your everyday life to make it more enjoyable. Tell yourself that nothing in life is boring! I suggest you take a first-time-attitude to you everyday life. That you constantly try to solve problems in a new, better and more enjoyable way.

ALWAYS SEE THROUGH FRESH EYES

Many years ago, I was at a lecture given by Mikael Andersson. Mikael was born without any arms or legs but, despite his handicap, Mikael has a normal job, children and drives just like everybody else, thanks to his specially designed car.

Mikael spoke about finding solutions to everyday problems. For him, even the most routine of tasks could be a big problem. Something which a person with two functioning arms and legs might call simple, like shaving your beard with a razor, was a real challenge for Mikael the first time he was faced with it. He described how he was supposed to go to an exhibition and present different types of aids for disabled people. Just before his trip, Mikael's electric razor was stolen and, because he hadn't the time to buy a new one, he decided to buy a manual razor and foam instead.

As you can imagine, it took him a long time to shave with the manual razor without any arms or hands. He explained that the most difficult part was getting the foam from the canister – how do you do this without arms? After many failed and messy attempts, he realised he could use the foam that had squirted out all over the hotel bed and the rest of the room. He lay his neck onto the spilled foam and eventually had enough on his face to allow him to shave.

The next problem was the manual razor – how could he hold it without hands? Because Mikael was used to encountering everyday challenges and finding innovative solutions, he finally managed to jam the razor against the washbasin and move his face against the razor, rather than the other way around. When Mikael turned up at the exhibition, his colleagues wondered if he had been in a fight, as his face was covered in cuts.

Mikael has become used to looking at problems differently to how most others do. His message to us in the audience, was to learn to see problems differently and try new ways of finding solutions.

If you grow up with fully functioning arms and legs, it can be difficult to identify with Mikael. Most of us are used to easily doing the things Mikael, or others with physical disabilities, find immensely difficult. We rarely have to step back and question the things we do routinely. We just shave ourselves, whilst people like Mikael must think: "*How* shall I shave myself?". The act of shaving with a manual razor highlights just one of the obstacles Mikael has had to learn to overcome. As a child, how can you play with kids of your own age, if you have no arms or legs? How do you take part in gymnastics at school? How do you even answer the telephone if you have no arms?

You might argue that Mikael has been forced into personal development. In order to live his life, he has needed to think in an entirely different way. Through his strong will, he has overcome his obstacles and come out a winner, and he can be a role model to all of us, regardless of our own physical or mental obstacles. Maybe you don't have such obvious obstacles as Mikael, but you have the same opportunities to develop. To succeed, you must challenge what you can and cannot do, erase the limitations of what is possible or impossible and dare to try things that you always thought were unreachable or difficult to achieve.

CHAPTER 3
EXPECTATIONS AND GOALS

Service to those around you is the rent you pay for your room on earth.
– Les Brown

The lecturer Les Brown, spoke once about the Dead Sea and why it was dead. He said it's because there is no fresh water flowing in from rivers or streams. It is the same water that remains there all the time, it never flows out. That's why it is dead. He suggested that we can see the same thing happen to us as human beings. If we don't add something new and fresh to our lives, or that of others, in the form of development, we die inside. The same connection can be seen with companies that stop in their own development and stand still, this is the first sign of their deaths.

A man without a goal is like a ship without a rudder.
– Thomas Carlyle

WHAT IS YOUR GOAL IN LIFE?

Regardless of age, you need to have both short- and long-term goals if you want to continue to develop and be successful. Some classic questions posed during job interviews include: Where do you see yourself in five years? What will you be doing in five years? In ten years? In twenty years? In one hundred and fifty years? Yes, your read that correctly, in one hundred and fifty years, what will you have achieved by then? You might think I'm mad; why should you set yourself a goal for long after you are dead, presuming you don't plan to reach that ripe old age? What do you think? Think about it for a while.

Everyday life seems pretty small when you start thinking one hundred and fifty years forward, doesn't it? Paying your bills becomes a triviality. Why should you have such long-term goals and how could you possibly implement them? Having a long-term focus, and having the amazing feeling that I may be able to influence something even after I am dead and buried, really motivates me. Imagine starting a foundation that can help X to achieve Y. If the foundation is managed correctly, it will continue to do the work you started and uphold the values you instilled in it. In this way, you and your ideals will continue to live long after you are gone. An exciting thought, right?

What footprints do you want to leave behind on earth?

Don't be afraid of setting earth-shattering, innovative goals. Ignore what others think is possible or not. If you want to fulfil something badly enough, you'll do it!

EXPECT SUCCESS

Whether you think that you can, or that you can't, you are usually right.
– Henry Ford

Consider this quote again: "Whether you think that you can, or that you can't, you are usually right". This has a really deep meaning. It means that if you say that you can do something, you can. If you say you can't, you probably won't. It is a self-fulfilling prophecy – whatever you think and believe, this will be your reality. It applies to all aspects of your life; success in your love life, your professional career, or in the sports you practice.

Another notable quote is from Dale Carnegie: "You can think yourself into defeat and misery, but you can also think yourself into success and happiness".

In the first chapter, we spoke about mentally visualising a specific event to ease the way to your goals. By doing this, you create an expectation that it will go well, that it will develop you, that you will learn from it or that you'll set a new record. When you create an expectation, it will be imprinted on you. It will look like you are waiting for something great to happen. Some might call this charisma. You get a glint in your eye that says you will get to where you want to go. Expect success, then success will follow – through yourself and through others!

COMMUNICATE YOUR GOAL

As I mentioned earlier, we all have different ways of looking at the outside world. Sometimes conflicts and misunderstandings arise, because one or more of the parties have not been sufficiently clear with their views and perspectives in a particular situation. I'd like to tell you two stories to highlight how things can go very wrong when there is a breakdown in the communication.

Once, there was a family who wanted to go on holiday to Abilene, where they had been every summer for the past three years. When they'd been on the road for a while, the husband turned to his wife and said: "It'll be fun to go to Abilene again, won't it? You've been looking forward to it for some time".

But this year, the wife decided she was going to be honest, and say what she really felt, so she replied: "No, not really. I just want to go because you want to go, you've been talking about it all year".

The husband was taken aback and turned to his children in the back of the car, and asked his son: "You think it'll be fun to go to Abilene, don't you?"

The son replied: "Well, I just go where you want to go."

"What about you", said the husband to his daughter, "you've been really looking forward to this trip, haven't you?"

She responded: "I'd rather stay at home and hang out with my friends."

So the husband said: "But I don't want to go to Abilene at all, I just thought it was you lot who wanted to go!"

Another example is about an old married couple who ate breakfast together in the same way they had done for years. Each morning, the man sliced his bread roll in two. He gave the bottom half to his wife and kept the top half for himself. One morning, the wife complained: "Typical! I get the bottom half again!" So the husband asked: "Don't you like the bottom half?" She said: "No, I much prefer the top half!" The husband replied: "But I don't even like the top half, I've always eaten it because I thought you liked the bottom half better!"

What can we learn from these stories about the trip to Abilene and the breakfast rolls?

If we don't communicate properly within our family, at work or amongst our friends, we come to believe that we all have the same picture within a situation and that everyone is happy. For the family that went on holiday, it took three years before they told one another what they really thought of their choice of destination. For the older couple, it took them many more years before they finally said how they enjoyed their breakfast rolls.

Don't wait for others to eventually read your mind, and don't assume that they want something that hasn't been explicitly expressed. Talk about everything with one another and don't hold back your opinions, trying to be kind. As the author and film director, Kay Pollak says: "Being someone's doormat is never an act of love".

In the workplace, it is easy to believe that everybody in the group has the same understanding of the organisational goals and visions. But often this is not the case, because everybody has their own view of their environment. There is no shared, communal view of anything in our world, and if we don't explain to one another how we understand things, it is a perfect breeding ground for misunderstandings. To create a common picture of a company's goals and visions, it is necessary to discuss and agree on a way of interpreting them.

If you are a leader of some kind, it is important that you gather your personnel and create a common picture of what it is you want to achieve. Don't do as the family who drove to Abilene did, or the old couple who shared their bread roll. Stop to say which way you want to go, instead of believing you are on the right track, only to discover, far too late, that you are going in opposite directions.

REALISE YOUR DREAMS

Now is the time that life is mine, this is my time on earth.
  – Gabriella's song, As it is in Heaven

For two and a half years, I was employed by a manpower agency. During that time, I worked in around thirty different workplaces. I met many different people and my persistent curiosity and thirst for knowledge drove me to ask them many searching questions. Questions like: Why do you work here? What are you going to do with your life? What would you do if you won one million dollars on the lottery?

Many people described how they had dreams that they would like to pursue, if only they had the money from a lottery win or such. They spoke of opening their own café, hairdressing salon or some other venture. With some of the people I met, I delved even further with some more motivational questions. Questions which often challenged their basic values and sometimes caused them to be anxious. But they also generated change.

I recall one particular workplace which had a very open, friendly and welcoming climate. Here, people often spoke in the canteen about fulfilling their dreams and goals. A few days after having such a conversation with a work colleague, he came to me and explained how he had applied to do a course to become a production manager. It was something he'd dreamed of for many years, but he had somehow found himself settled into a comfortable way of life where the days just went on, almost automatically. He hadn't stopped to challenged himself and his life, until I awakened this idea within him. A couple of weeks later, he received a call from the school he'd applied to, saying that he'd successfully secured a place on the next course, and he thanked me again for giving him the motivation he needed to apply for the course and change his life's direction.

The important thing with this story, is that it was not me who pushed him closer to achieving his dream – he did that himself. The only thing I did was ask a few questions about his dreams. I poked him and awoke him from his slumber.

Throughout life most of us have a number of biological alarm clocks which are thought to awaken something in us. These are the mid-life crises which occur at thirty, forty and fifty years of age and so on. Not everyone awakes to these alarms, but instead ignore them and continue dozing. By asking yourself the right questions, you don't need to wait for a midlife crisis to create a change in your view of life and what you achieve from the only life you have here on earth.

SETTING A GOAL

What does it take to create a change in your life? Setting goals for what you want to achieve within the various elements of your life, is an important part of generating change. When setting goals, there are various things to consider. The six-point list below, is taken from Napoleon Hill's book, *Think and Grow Rich.* The book refers to financial success but, of course, can be tailored to achieving whichever type of goal you please.

1. Decide exactly the amount of money you want to have. Don't just say that you want lots of money, but give an exact sum.

2. Decide what you are willing to give up to get the money you want. There is no such thing as "something for nothing".

3. Decide a date when you will have this money in your hand.

4. Decide on a specific plan of how you will achieve your wish, and get started right away, whether you are prepared or not.

5. Write down on a piece of paper exactly how much money you want, when you want it and describe in detail what you are prepared to do to get it (points 1–4).

6. Read out loud to yourself what you have written, twice a day. Once when you get up in the morning, and once before you go to bed. As you read, you tell yourself that you already have the money.

FOCUS ON YOUR GOAL

It's in your moments of decisions that your destiny is shaped ... Choose wisely! – Tony Robbins

By setting yourself goals, you put your subconscious to work. Your subconscious is like a slave who just does what it's told. When you set goals, and engage yourself emotionally to achieve them, you tell your subconscious that this is what you want to achieve and, all day and night, it will help you find ways of achieving it. A goal which is clear will also help you make decisions which will bring you closer to achieving it.

Each day, you are faced with different decisions, or "crossroads" if you prefer. The decision you make leads you either closer to your goal or further from it. Imagine that you find yourself in the Now on the picture that follows, and that you want to reach your Goal. By remaining focussed on your goal, you will make decisions based upon achieving it, and the likelihood that you will choose the paths that lead there will increase. Your choices will eventually determine whether you reach your goal or not.

Imagine that your goal is to lose a certain amount of weight. If you really want, with all your heart, to lose weight, you will feel guilty when you eat a cake or something else unhealthy. By choosing to eat the cake, you choose one pathway and by choosing not to eat it, you choose another. Which is the right way to go to achieve your goal?

Your entire journey towards reaching your goal is made up of crossroads, and it is through your choice of pathway that you create the future you are searching for. By applying this to weight loss, you can break the goal down into the choices you make each day. Decide that, until you reach your target, you will only have a cup of unsweetened coffee without cake during a coffee break. That you will park your car one block further down the street from work, that you will get off the bus one stop earlier, go for a brisk walk during your lunch break, and so on.

Of course, it sometimes happens that you get lost and take the wrong pathway. Then it is important to find your way back, to choose the right way again and continue your journey towards your goal. I hope you are starting to see the connection between the small choices and the ultimate achievement of your goals. Small steps or decisions each day are what create the results you desire. Each day, I make small choices which help me move forwards, everything from choosing the stairs instead of the lift, to following up small ideas which come to me and then realising them.

SEE AND TOUCH YOUR GOAL

What is your goal? Buying a new car? Having a big wedding? Building your own house? Becoming a successful musician?

If you really want to achieve a given goal, your entire way of thinking will be affected by your ambition to reach it. Regardless of your goal, you will need to enforce the feeling of wanting to reach it. A good trick for maintaining your motivation to keep working towards your goal is to see and feel it whenever you begin to question it. If your goal is to buy a new car, go and look at it, test drive it, take pictures of it. Put the pictures up at home – the mirror in the bathroom is an effective place! This will ensure you keep the spark alive until you reach your goal.

A MAGIC POWER

Have you ever decided to attain a certain goal and started to work towards it? Perhaps you felt unsure to begin with about whether you would succeed. Have you experienced uncertainty when talking about your goals with friends and other people? Have you, after a while, started to believe in your goal and you no longer have a problem talking with other people about it? Have you experienced that, in time, you start to believe and be convinced that you will reach the goal, that there is no longer anything stopping you from succeeding? If you have not yet experienced this, you will do if you find a goal that you really want to achieve with all your heart.

There are four steps on the road to achieving the magical power within you that will help you succeed:

1. You search for a goal. When you discover what it is, write it down and think about it whenever you can.

2. You become unsure. You don't always have the courage to tell other people about your goals and plans. Don't give up here if people criticise your plans.

3. You start to believe. Now, you are ready to tell people what you want to achieve and you no longer care about what people say or think.

4. You become totally convinced. No problem is beyond your capabilities. Regardless of how many dream thieves (see chapter 5) you come across, you will shake off their comments and move on, you are unstoppable! You will succeed.

It is in the last phase, peculiar things begin to happen. Things that can be perceived as impossible and almost supernatural. You are thinking about a certain person and suddenly you will receive a phone call from that person. You get an unexpected windfall which helps you continue towards your goal. You meet people who want to help you reach your goal. You see possibilities in all situations. You are determined to reach your goal and achieve the success that you truly deserve!

Next time you decide to reach a particular goal, bare this in mind: when you reach a certain point, there is no going back, and you cannot fail. If you have visualised yourself reaching a goal, you will get there!

YOUR GOALS

Take a second and think back to your childhood. Christmas is around the corner, and you are sitting on the floor, playing. Your parents sit down next to you and ask what you would like for Christmas. I don't think any child would limit their wishes by thinking: "it is too expensive" or "there is no point in asking for that, I will tire of it soon anyway". No, you probably asked for the thing that you wanted most of all, regardless of whether it was actually possible or not.

The same thing applies to adults, we can still ask for anything we want. And when you write down what you want to have or experience, and start thinking about how to achieve it, that wish will become a goal to work towards. So, think about the following questions and write down your answers. Take your time:

» What do I really want from my life?

» What do I need to achieve so I can look back on my life when I am old and be proud of my achievements?

» What goal do I want to achieve in three weeks?

» What goal do I want to achieve in three months?

» What goal do I want to achieve in three years?

» What goal do I want to achieve in thirty years?

» What goal do I want to achieve in on hundred and thirty years?

» What is stopping me from achieving my goals?

CHAPTER 4
GETTING THINGS DONE

I can determine whether you will be successful or not by your way of managing time.
– Mike Murdock

Did you know that you have one special thing in common with Bill Gates, Microsoft's founder? Time. You both have exactly the same amount of time every day, every week, every year. So, what is it that makes him a multi-millionaire but not you (yet)? He has learned to plan his time and to respect it. It is said that time is more valuable than money. You can always get more money, but you can never get time back.

A RESOURCE FOR GETTING THE RIGHT THINGS DONE

Time is a fair resource in life. Everyone has the same amount; twenty four hours each day, sixty minutes each hour. The difference lies in what we do with that time. Regardless of what you are doing, there are things that you don't have time for because other, unimportant, stuff gets in the way. I want to share a way of prioritising what needs to be done. It is a technique that I have used many times with good results.

Do the following:
1. Write down the things you need to do.
2. Put a number 1 in front of the most important task, a number 2 in front of the second most important task and continue to prioritise down to the last item.

3. When you start working with your tasks, go through them according to the order of priority. Stay with each task until it is completed or until you reach an obstacle and cannot continue right away. Then continue with the next task on the priority list.

There are many advantages with this method of structuring. Should you only have time for three tasks on your list, they will still be the tasks you feel are most important, the less important will have to wait. You will also notice a significant difference in your way of working, and your efficiency. Your stress will decrease dramatically. After all, now you only have one thing to think about, instead of ten all at the same time.

A SCHEDULE IN BLOCKS

Lecturer Bob Harrison talks in one of his courses about "time management" and about how you should plan your time according to the planned result of the activity. This course has helped me to choose what to dedicate my time to. Bob Harrison uses three terms to make prioritising easier: Hipos, Lopos and Nopos.

Hipos: High Payoffs.

Lopos: Low Payoffs.

Nopos: No Payoffs.

Imagine a schedule of blocks, either half hours or hours, and you have the possibility to move those blocks around in your schedule. The idea of seeing your schedule as blocks is that you improve your flexibility and are able to move the blocks around when needed, such as when something unexpected happens.

When you plan your time, ask yourself: How will this payoff? Take away all the time-consuming activities which do not give a high payoff. By prioritising activities that are Hipos, you will get the most important things done first. When you have time left over, you can engage in your Lopos activities and if you have even more time to spare, you can engage in your Nopos, which could be washing the dishes. As long as there are clean plates, washing the dishes will not give any payoff, but when you run out of clean plates, washing the dishes will suddenly become a Hipo in order for you to eat.

You can arrange for some Lopos and Nopos to give more time for Hipos. For example, you could buy a dishwasher so you won't have to spend time on washing up by hand. My wife and I bought a dishwasher so we could free up time for other things. Since neither of us like washing up, this was one of the best investments we ever made. Now we no longer have discussions about whose turn it is to wash up and we are free to do other things instead.

DEVELOP A HABIT

The road to the start line is the longest.
 – Arne Hirdman

There are many theories about how long it takes to develop a good habit or a bad habit. Some say it takes ten days, while others say thirty. Regardless, there are many tricks to more easily develop good habits. One trick is to use the six-point list from Chapter 2. By having a well-defined goal, it is easier to stay motivated when you want to create a new habit.

You can also reinforce your new behaviours by rewarding yourself immediately afterwards. This subconsciously creates a positive association with your new habit, which helps you towards your goal. When you get a good feeling afterwards, you are encouraged to continue with your new behaviour.

To break a pattern and create a new habit, you need to avoid your old habits, and anything associated with them. If you have set a goal that you will, rather than watch television every evening, read a good book, you should avoid reading in your favourite TV chair. Your subconscious has already associated the chair with watching TV, which will remind you that you want to watch TV and hence you will lose focus on your reading.

To create a change, you must also have a positive and supportive inner conversation. The change itself can be done in a second. For example: "I have decided not to get annoyed if someone cuts in front of me when I'm driving in traffic". BANG! Now you have changed. What takes time when engaging in long-term change, is preparing yourself mentally. One step in this mental preparation is to tell yourself that you want the change and that it is actually good for you.

DOING IT NOW OR LATER

Countless times I have heard people who want to lose weight say that they'll start after the holidays, once everything is over. Why? As you probably already know, it´s quite easy to postpone things that you would rather avoid, even if you know that you need to do it. So, what is the danger with this? In losing weight, it is very likely that you will take the opportunity to have a little more to eat now before starting the diet. What will happen then? Well, there will be more weight to lose. Why not start straight away and avoid the extra kilos?

Start today, skip the cake. Choose the pathway that we spoke about earlier. Choose the right path straight away, then you will reach your goal quicker and reach your desired weight. The same thing goes for those uncomfortable phone calls that you would rather not make. Instead of being nervous and delaying the call, do what lecturer Richard Bandler says. Dial the number. Once the phone is ringing, you can start worrying. It is already too late by then anyway. It works really well and your phone call will be over with.

SATISFACTION GIVES BETTER RESULTS

There is a theory created by Abraham Maslow which describes our human needs, called *Maslow's hierarchy of needs*. During my studies and in writing this book, I have noticed that his theory fits well into my own life. Namely, that you must satisfy certain basic needs before you can be constructive, creative and reach self-actualisation, in my case being able to write books. Below follows a description of the different levels of satisfaction. Bear in mind that, according to Maslow, every step must be fulfilled before you can climb onto the next step before we reach self-actualisation where you perform at the top of your game and feel great.

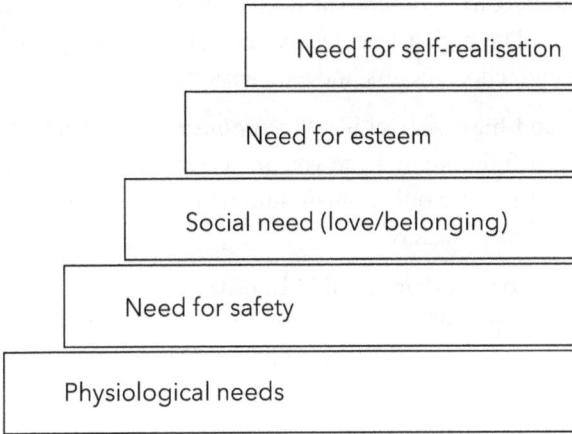

Maslow's Hierarchy of Needs

1. The first level you need to satisfy, just in order to survive, are the basic *physiological* needs. Examples include food, sleep and warmth. Even sex according to some researchers.

2. The second level is the need for *safety*. This includes both physical and emotional safety and we reach this level only once the first level is satisfied. Here, some people feel the need to create structure and order around themselves. At this level, we feel worry and anxiety for all sorts of things around us unless we have our need of safety satisfied.

3. The third level is the social need for *love/belonging*. This level emphasises the need for friendship, being in love, the feeling of belonging to social groups and having emotional ties to other people. A lack of social acknowledgement creates an anxiety which is mostly satisfied through marriage, membership of different clubs or organisations, or by belonging in different groups.

4. The fourth level is the need for *esteem*, status or prestige. There are

two different level to satisfy. The lower level which deals with your need for respect from others, the need of power, honour, fame and dominance. The higher level means resect for yourself, self-confidence, competence, success, independence and freedom.

5. The fifth and highest level is *self-actualisation*. At this level, you live out your full potential and you are a creative force. According to Maslow, there are only a small number of people who have the capacity to reach this level.

How does this theory work in real life? In order to connect it to reality, I will give an example of the times I have studied for an exam at the university. When I planned my study time, I had Maslow's Hierarchy of Needs in mind, so I could create the conditions needed to get as high up in the hierarchy model as possible. To satisfy the first level, I ensured that I had plenty of sleep the night before. I ate good, healthy food and wore the right clothes so that I wouldn't lose focus by being too hot or too cold. My aim was to dress so that I could easily vary my clothes, depending upon the temperature of the place.

To reach the second level, safety, I made sure I did not have any unresolved conflicts or other important details in my head which might disrupt my focus. In my case, I found safety through my relationship with my wife. When we parted in the morning, I made sure our relationship was as good as it could possibly be, which gave me strength throughout the day.

To fulfil the social need, I used to sit at the university and study. That way, I had a feeling of belonging, since I enjoyed being in an environment with other students around me. Everyone there had the same goal; to develop, learn new things and get some sort of qualification.

The fourth level, I satisfied through personal development by respecting other people and myself. To satisfy this level, I thought back to earlier situations where I have made a success of something and I tried to reinforce the same feeling when I wanted to achieve something in the here and now. In some cases, I even looked up people who I could be reinforced through, like the nice lady in the university canteen.

By working with all of the different levels on the same day that I had to study or complete an exam, I created the conditions I needed to be creative and self-actualised in my way of thinking.

DON'T FIGHT ON TOO MANY FRONTS AT THE SAME TIME

As I mentioned earlier, I am absolutely convinced that we cannot do a decent job unless we learn how to focus on one thing at a time. Our conscious part of the brain cannot, according to scientists, concentrate on more than one thought, which means that we can only think of one thing at a time. However, we can think of one thing, start thinking about another, jump back to the first thought, and so on. Since this happens so quickly, you will probably not notice it. Perhaps you notice that you "lose the thread" if someone asks you a question. So, when in a situation where you need to get something demanding done, it is important to let go of all other thoughts that might disturb you.

Let us say that you know you have bills that are late and need to be paid, but you also know that you have something at work which needs to be done before the next day in order for you to keep within your work schedule. When you are working, you will continually be distracted by knowing that you have bills which need to be paid and will lose focus on your job. In a situation such as this, I would recommend that you pay your bills first and then concentrate on your work. Maybe you will think that you then won't have time to do your work, but bear in mind that if you ensure you satisfy all distracting factors first, your brain will be far more efficient and you will be able to concentrate all of your power on work. For me, this has been important so I can gather the strength I need to complete the task before me. You should try it too, and see if you notice any difference.

CHAPTER 5
TAKING FULL RESPONSIBILITY IN LIFE

THINKING LIKE A CHILD OR AN ADULT

What does it mean to you, to take full responsibility for your life? Is it as an unknown source wrote: "To 'take responsibility' in today's society is a new way for politicians to say sorry, but not to take any of the consequences..."

As children, we are trouble-free and normally have nothing to seriously worry us. We mostly run around having fun and playing. As adults, we are considerably more worried about things and have many more problems. Sometimes important things, like how to pay the rent, and sometimes less important such as what will the neighbours say if I paint the house red.

Sometimes you illustrate your step from being a child to an adult with two cliff edges on either side of a precipice that you need to jump over. Going from being someone who takes no responsibility to being someone who takes full responsibility, is not always as simple as it might seem. Many people find it difficult to take the giant leap needed to get over to the grown-up side where you take the full responsibility. Many people get stuck between the rocks and set up home in Whinge City. From the outside, Whinge City works exactly like the rest of society, but in Whinge City it is fully accepted to pass responsibility to other people and to not take accountability for your own actions and thoughts.

Examples of opinions which are commonplace in Whinge City include: "What rubbish weather we have. We pay too much tax. Our politicians are hopeless. I'm fat, but it is inherited and in my genes. Why should I be cheerful and do my job well, it's Friday after all. The goalkeeper was hopeless, he let in three goals yesterday. It's not my fault I got involved in crime, it is because I had a bad childhood".

In Whinge City, there is a lot of whinging, hence the name. They blame others for things that go wrong, and never themselves. Whenever I run into these people, I ask them something along the lines of: "Interesting. What are *you* going to do about it?" That normally stops them in their tracks because they are not normally used to thinking that they should solve or change the problems that they are complaining about. Just like a small child, they haven't yet learned to take responsibility for their actions and situations. I hope that you now see the difference between being a child and being an adult. To take responsibility and do something, instead of sitting in the crowd, complaining about a bad game. You are the game, you are the one who decides how your life will turn out, no-one else.

Just to be clear, don't mistake being adult and responsible with losing your childishness. Quite the opposite, an adult who has maintained a sense of childishness can still joke and have fun, but will take the consequences for the joke if it does not go as planned.

DON'T THROW BLAME AROUND

Blame is a common way of moving your own flaws onto somebody else instead. A person who feels good about themselves seldom has the need to try and blame others. The way I see it, there are three types of personality when we talk about blame. One who blames others, one who is on the receiving end of blame, and one who is blame-free and does not use blame in his or her life. The person who blames others uses blame to influence others and get them to think, feel or do things in a certain way. Some examples of attempts at blaming, is when one partner in a relationship asks the other if he or she might go out for a drink with friends. The answer could then be something like: "Well, I guess I'll just sit at home alone tonight then…" or another situation "if you do x, I will feel y". Therefore, the blamer takes no responsibility for his feelings but instead likes to see himself as a victim and uses this to influence his surroundings. If you find yourself to be a blamer, you need to evaluate if it's really worth it, and if there is anything inside of you that you need to work on, in order to stop manipulating others using blame as a tool. Influencing people through feelings of blame does not work in the long run and will often lead to negative feelings for the person blaming others. Nobody likes a person who you constantly feel sorry for and that must be constantly appeased.

The person on the receiving end of the blame, allows himself to be influenced by the person doing the blaming. The blamer gets the receiver to do things they do not want to do, such as staying home from a party they would have liked to have gone to. All this because the blamer whinges about having to sit home alone for some, probably made-up, reason. A person receiving blame can put in overtime at work, just because his boss blamed him and he feels forced to stay late to complete what his boss thinks he should have had time to finish.

A person who is blame-free has been able to see through the blame-game and decided not to be a part of it. This person takes responsibility for his own thoughts and feelings and deals with them inside himself, instead of trying to put the blame on someone else. Every time somebody tries to blame them, they will say something like: "You're not trying to make me feel bad, are you? It is not going to work!" By saying this straight out, they will remove the power from the blame-thrower's attempt at blaming them and they will remain with no feelings of blame.

It is said that we always look for the opposite of ourselves when we fall in love, and this is frighteningly often how we deal with blame too. A blame-thrower, or a person who blames others, looks for a blame-receiver so that that he can misuse his power in the shape of blaming someone else. The couple will then comprise one person who blames and one receiving the blame. They will have children and will raise new blame-throwers and blame-receivers. If both partners instead become aware of the blame throwing and learn how to be blame-free, the relationship will be more harmonious without the daily conflict that blame-throwing brings.

Practice becoming aware of if you are trying to blame another person for something that is really about you and your feelings. Also, practice trying to recognise when someone else is trying to use blame as a tool of power against you, and make the person aware that it doesn't work and that this person has a responsibility to deal with his own feelings.

EXCUSES

Does it ever happen that you are late for meetings at work or with friends? What do you usually use as an excuse for being late? "Sorry for being late, but I missed the bus" or "there was a lot of traffic on the motorway again". When did you last use an excuse such as: "I'm sorry for being late, but I was over-optimistic with my planning and I really thought I would make it on time and that there would be no queue on the motorway. I simply left home too late".

What is the difference in these two types of apology? In the last one you chose to take a personal responsibility for your actions instead of blaming other circumstances. Regardless of how you look at it, the reason that you were late was that you made a number of choices that led to you not making it on time. You chose not to leave earlier, even though you knew that there is often a lot of traffic on the motorway at that time of day, you clearly left too late if you missed the bus, and so on. In other words, it is up to you if you make it on time or not. Some people say it is a lack of respect for the person you are meeting not to make it on time without letting them know or without having a good excuse. For other people, "it doesn't really matter". What excuses do you use in your daily life and what excuses do other people use on you?

DREAM THIEVES

On the road to success you will meet many people who do not want the best for you. As soon as you have made the decision to jump over to the grown-ups' cliff and take responsibility for your own life and future, you will notice changes in people around you. Even your closest friends and family may start to treat you differently.

Those who haven't made the leap themselves and are still on the cliff of no responsibility, or have set up home in Whinge City, will be jealous and try to pull you back. These people are called dream thieves and they will do anything in their power to pull you back when you have become successful in your life, regardless of what that success looks like.

If you have decided to lose weight and have started a new lifestyle, your heavier friends will either follow you and start a weight-loss journey of their own, or they will try to pull you down. Maybe they will invite you home for a coffee and have your favourite cakes out because, consciously or subconsciously, they do not want you to succeed. Because as soon as you succeed, you will prove to them and others around them that it is possible to change your lifestyle. If they are not ready to do the same change, you have proven how much more successful you are in reaching your goals, which will be hard for them to accept and they will no longer have an excuse for, in this case, their weight problem. If they do not succeed in pushing you down, some "friends" will choose to distance themselves from you.

Learn to identify who around you wants to support you, and who would rather try to break you when you have decided to reach a goal. Avoid spending time with those who do not want to see you succeed – if there are enough of them, sooner or later they will succeed in pulling you down and you will fail in reaching your goal. Look at yourself as a battery; some people will charge you, and some will discharge you and take all your energy. Make a conscious choice to spend more time with people who charge you. That way you will have more energy left over to live your life!

CHAPTER 6
PEOPLE SENT TO TEST YOU

If you're annoyed by the things that are small, I guess you're no bigger than them after all.
  – Alf Henriksson

My reasoning in this chapter has been greatly inspired by the lecturer and film director, Kay Pollak. His teachings have greatly affected my way of thinking and being.

THE POSSIBILITY TO CHOOSE YOUR MOOD

Did you know you are able to choose your mood? Depending on how you deal with a certain situation and how you direct your thoughts, you can choose if you want to become a victim or become a fully responsible human being directing your own mood. It is a choice we are faced with many times every day. In the morning when you wake up you choose whether to feel sorry for yourself for having to get up, or whether to jump up and say: "This will be a wonderful day!" The choice is yours.

If you, for example, are unhappy with your job – do something about it instead of complaining. If you forget yourself and become a victim, remind yourself by saying: "Hang on a minute, I am responsible for my own thoughts!" The rest of the day, you will be tested many times and you will have many opportunities to choose responsibility instead of giving yourself the role of a victim.

If someone or something succeeds in disturbing you and makes you lose focus, it is important to reflect afterwards about why that happened. In most cases, the reason for losing your temper is a message from yourself that you can learn from. No person can make you lose your temper, it is only you yourself who chooses how to react to a situation. The question is: "Why did you choose to lose your temper?"

PEOPLE SENT TO TEST YOU

Have you ever met a person who, for no reason at all, acts towards you with a bad attitude or acts negatively towards you? Have you got a work colleague who is often moody or irritated at you? Do you have children or a partner who sometimes get you in a bad mood? Good! These are people who are "sent" to help you grow as a person. If we see ourselves as students of life, learning and becoming better, every obstacle will make us stronger. Every problem is an opportunity to learn something new about ourselves or our surroundings.

I have sometimes noticed that I have started to get along more with work colleagues just before they leave their position. If you adhere to this way of thinking, you could say that he or she is no longer sent to test you as you have learned to "deal with" him. Have you ever experienced this yourself? Once the person sent to test you disappears from your life, there will be new people sent to take their place. But you will never be tested more than you are able to deal with. Remember that!

PRACTICE BEING HUMBLE

If you decide to look at people as being sent to help you grow, your view of challenging and unpleasant people will slowly start to change. You will start to look at these people with gratitude for them being there. This is a completely new way of thinking and will need some training before it comes naturally. For this to come naturally, you need to feel it in your bones, or as psychologists say: that you have trained it into your subconscious which drives your actions when you are not 100% mentally present.

I have wondered about which types of situations cause me to become annoyed at trivial things. Most often it is in traffic. Let me give you an example: You are at a crossroads in your car when another car approaches. You choose to stop and wait for it to pass. Just before it passes, it makes a turn without indicating, and you have stood there waiting for what seems like a very long time. I still sometimes reach for the horn to show my anger at the person for not indicating, but I manage to stop myself at the last moment.

Is it really necessary to get upset in this situation? The answer is no. It is very rarely necessary to be upset about anything. Choose instead to see the other driver as having been sent to try you, and think something along the lines of: "How good, someone who has been sent to try me" or "Thank you, how kind of you to try me". Who knows, maybe the driver did indicate, but did not know that his light bulb was broken. He is hardly going to be upset when he exits the crossroads, so why should you be. Ask yourself what you have to gain from being angry at the driver or anyone else who tests your patience. The answer to the question is usually: nothing.

DON'T BECOME SELF-SACRIFICING

Kay Pollak warns us not to go too far when being humble, as this soon becomes self-sacrificing. I believe you should be able to get angry and put your foot down sometimes, otherwise your humility can get used by people against you. As Kay says: "Being somebody else's doormat is never an act of love". This is true. Living a life where you become less worthy, so that you can be humble towards, say, your partner, is not healthy. In a relationship, both partners have the same right to live their life to the full, and to have a relationship where one partner uses the other is often destructive for at least one of the partners.

Of course, it can be hard to live in complete equal balance all the time. Sometimes one of you may be more successful at work or in a sport, which will lead to the other person taking on a supporting role and holding back on their dreams. But it must never spill over into using the other partner's good intentions. Find a balance so you are not made to feel smaller without valid reasons. You have only one life to live and cannot be made to live that life solely for somebody else.

The same thing can be said about your workplace. Don't let your colleagues push you down, walk all over and make your work miserable. Stand up for yourself, there is a limit to the number of people sent to try you so don't accept them all. No-one has the right to use you by profiting from the humility you have developed in yourself. You yourself choose how many people sent to try you are taken on. Remember that.

WHAT WILL BE WILL BE

Do you believe in fate? That things happen for a reason? That there is a reason for everything that happens? I do. However, it is not always obvious what the reason is and we do not always find out. For example, when loved ones die we often have great difficulty in seeing the purpose of it.

Whether or not you believe in fate, I am convinced that an effective way of thinking and dealing with different situations in life, is to look at it as meant to be. In most cases, I can see afterwards why fate stirred things up.

For example: Once I was due to meet a woman to talk about a lecture I was due to give at a university. She called me two days before the meeting and re-scheduled it for a week later. I didn't mind because I had honestly not prepared very well. A couple of days later, I had a eureka moment. I would of course present to her a whole concept of lectures, instead of just the one. I started working with the concept and planned several lectures which I presented to her. Had I met her at the original time, I would probably have given my one lecture and never developed my broader concept. It is hard for me not to believe that her getting in touch and re-scheduling the meeting was *meant to be*. And this is just one example which has made me realise that every person I meet, every situation I am exposed to is there to teach me something, and I am to seize these opportunities.

SEE THE WORLD AROUND YOU AS YOUR TEACHER

Do you think you know everything, just because you graduated from school or recently completed a course at work? I hope you are still open to new impressions and want to learn more and see things from other viewpoints and gain new insights. "Every day is a school day" is an old cliché and, in my case, this really is true. Since my great passion is learning how to understand people, every meeting I have is rewarding, and being with people allows me to learn new things each day.

Even though I am the author of this book, I am not saying that everything I have experienced and written fits with your life and experiences. If your experiences about something I have written differ from mine, please tell me next time we meet. Regardless of how young or old you are, you have experiences that the world will benefit from. Les Brown says: "You are never too old to learn, and you are never too young to teach!"

EVERYONE DOES THEIR BEST

I had a rather strict upbringing. My father had learned from his parents that children were to be physically disciplined if they did not obey. Most people today agree that this is completely wrong, but he did what he thought was right. He didn't reflect over his way of bringing me up, but instead acted as his parents had done to him. This phenomenon is called the social inheritance. For many years I was angry with him and we had no contact.

At one point, I listened to an audio book about personal development where the message was to forgive your parents. I listened to the book several times until I eventually understood that my father had just done what he thought was best. He didn't know any better.

Sometimes we meet people who we find it difficult to socialise or work with because we think they behave stupidly, are sloppy or slow. As soon as you get irritated with someone, remember that they do the best they can from the resources they have. This is a disarming action which will help you to maintain your patience.

CHAPTER 7
AN INNER CONVERSATION

Do you have an internal dialogue in your mind? According to many researchers, that's completely normal. During a study I carried out when studying psychology, I posed the same question to forty people in an anonymous survey. I was interested to see if the ability to being aware of an internal dialogue was something which developed over many years or whether it was congenital, so I chose to ask both young people and senior citizens. A clear majority claimed to hear these inner voices amongst both age groups. The next question I asked, was whether inner conversation could control their actions? Again, a clear majority said that they felt guided by their voices and inner conversation.

What can we learn from the results of my survey? Well, the inner conversation affects what we do and how we think. If that many people hear and follow their inner conversation, we can only hope that these voices are saying the right things and helping them to develop. I have an active internal conversation myself and had never reflected over this until I began to learn about personal development.

I think there is a connection between hearing voices and having strong instincts, listening to yourself and your inner thoughts. The subconscious part of the brain works like a slave who only does as he is told. If we train our thoughts so that we think in a certain way, the subconscious part of the brain will follow.

Here is a good example of how to control your subconscious mind with the power of your inner thoughts. Imagine the following scenario: You are the captain of a large ship and on that ship you have sailors who do everything you tell them. As the captain, perhaps you say: "Hoist the sail!". Your sailors respond: "Aye aye, Captain!" and hoist the sail. In the same way, you are the captain of your subconscious. When you tell yourself: "I can't do this!", your "sailors" respond with "Aye aye, Captain!" and confirm your belief that you are not competent. This small confirmation can have a huge ripple effect if you do not break the thought and give a new order, saying that you are actually as competent and capable as you are. The next time you face a choice, your previous orders will tell your sailors how to act. If you see an advertisement for your dream job, the thought will come to you that: "I don't know enough about this type of work, I'm not competent enough to even stand a chance of getting it": Your sailors will respond with "Aye aye, Captain!" and you will really believe you cannot get your dream job even though you deserve it and actually have a pretty good chance of getting it.

To use this system positively, you must begin to give positive commands to your brain and it will then attempt to respond to these commands in order to achieve what you tell it. Become aware of the thoughts you send to your sailors, start sending them more positive commands and you will experience a tremendous change.

STAGE FRIGHT

Do you get nervous when you have to speak in front of a group of people? I have had, and sometime still do have, a problem standing in front of a large group and talking. Being afraid to speak in front of a group is quite normal and many of us have been unwillingly trained as children that it is frightening to stand in front of the class. At school, we were always encouraged to speak in front of the class about subjects which neither interested nor motivated us, which created a great deal of uncertainty within us. This uncertainty led to embarrassing presentations and created a negative association with standing in front of people. This negative association lives on in many of us, often long into adult life, and is hard to break.

I remember when I started working with teaching information technology at a secondary school, without having gained any formal teacher training. The pedagogic knowledge I had was gained from my officer training in the military. Even though there were some similarities, I cannot say that leading a platoon of soldiers in the field is the same as teaching a class of teenagers. I had to find new ways of dealing with my role as a teacher.

At the start, the classroom environment itself was a challenge. There were four groups of tables which formed small islands in the room. Because I was nervous about speaking in front of the whole class, I instead went around to each of the islands speaking to small groups of students at a time. It was not very efficient and I was constantly repeating myself. Because I wanted to become a better teacher and provide better lessons, I finally had to learn to speak in front of the whole class at the same time.

At first, it was difficult to speak to the whole class and this made me uncertain in my role. But, as I used a military approach to leadership, I soon became more confident because I'd had more experience exercising with soldiers in the field than being in a lecture theatre with a group of youngsters. My practice of speaking in front of the students made me better and better and after two years as a teacher I had not the slightest problem speaking in front of a class – in fact, I found it a lot of fun. I received positive feedback after my lectures and my exams showed that there was a measurable enhancement in knowledge amongst the students I had at the end of my period as a teacher when compared to when I first began two years earlier.

If you feel uneasy about your role or the topic you are speaking about, it is natural to feel nervous. But as soon as you become more comfortable in your role, you will become calmer and feel safer in yourself as a speaker. Practice is hard, to force yourself to train over and over again until it no longer feels difficult.

No matter how much you practice speaking, you can still sometimes find yourself in situations where you are unsure of yourself and what you are about to do. I am convinced we can trace it back to one important crucial factor: our inner conversation. Depending on the situation, these voices – or your inner conversation – tell you what to do and how to think, and that will affect the outcome.

It became very clear when I began with personal development and wanted to change my way of thinking. Before, I was an easily-irritated and seldom positive kind of person, but today I am happy and outgoing. I became like this through becoming aware of my inner conversation and actively trying to influence it and how I experienced different situations. It took a long time, but I have made a journey and I am grateful to my previous work colleague's choice to introduce me to personal development through the cassettes he loaned me and the lectures he took me to. I became aware of how much our inner conversation influences us, whether it is relating to stage fright, daring to apply for a dream job or achieving any other goal.

HOW DOES THE INNER CONVERSATION WORK?

If you have read Tintin, you will know that Captain Haddock hears two different voices when he is confronted with alcohol; the good voice and the bad one. The situations are often illustrated by him having an angel on one shoulder and the devil on the other. The angel and the devil argue over who will force their will upon him and eventually Captain Haddock chooses to listen to one of them. The same thing happens to you when you stand at the checkout in the shop and you receive too much change from the cashier. You can choose to listen to the good angel's voice and tell the cashier that you have received too much, or you can listen to the devil and keep the extra change. Ultimately there will be a dialogue in your mind where you consider whether to speak out or not.

If we think back to the fact that many people are steered by their inner voices, it is important to try to have positive voices that help us rather than voices that bring us down. Can you change your inner voice? Of course! How? Well, by constantly being aware of your inner conversation and acting like a police officer – arrest all the negative voices that pop up! You can correct your own thoughts by saying to yourself: "No, no, that's not right at all". It can be experienced as unusual and difficult to grasp, but it is worth it.

I remember when I first began listening to my inner conversations. It could be about anything: how bad I was at something, how unsuccessful I was or how others were lazy, strange or behaved badly. There were really no fun thoughts at all. I began training myself to steer my inner conversations and in this way actively chose how my thoughts would be. I had never thought it possible to choose how to think or that I could choose whether to be cheerful or angry, that I could change my mood in a second – but it turned out to be truly possible!

LEARN TO STEER YOUR INNER CONVERSATION

Step one in learning how to steer your inner conversation, is to actively listen to your thoughts and how they work. The next step is to open a discussion between the positive and negative. When I did this for the first time, it was a strange feeling breaking one's own thoughts and entering into this discussion. If someone else had been able to hear my thoughts they would have experienced them as a heated debate where everybody was fighting to have their voices heard. If my negative voice said something which the positive voice either couldn't or wouldn't defend, I would have to actively go in and suppress it. In the beginning, it became obvious – I literary had to think: "That's enough, I'm not interested in your opinion," or "it doesn't matter what you say, I know that I can do it anyway". When I'd done this a few times, the negative voice gradually subsided and the positive took more place in my thoughts. What followed was that whenever I was forced to make quick decisions, I began to choose more positive alternatives.

Having practiced this technique for several years, I now find it much easier to manage silly and negative thoughts. Now when a negative thought crops up, I can usually laugh it away and continue being happy, instead of falling victim to my own thoughts and being weighed down with aggression and negativity.

Before, I didn't much like the rain and didn't really enjoy being outside in it. This attitude changed when I completed my National Service in the Army in 1998. I was on sentry duty and my task was to stand at the front gate of my regiment and control entry. I'd forgotten to bring my waterproof clothing with me and, of course, it began to rain five minutes after taking position at my post. Because I was alone at my post, I didn't have the chance to go and get my waterproofs so, to cope with this situation, I made a decision – I decided that rain was fun! Something clicked inside me and, since then, I have always liked going out in the rain.

Next time you go out in weather which you don't much care for, listen to what your inner conversation says. Instead of running to the car or bus when it starts to rain – stop, put the umbrella away, look up at the sky and say with a smile: "What nice weather it is!" Just saying the words out loud generates a reaction in your body which reacts to what you say by spreading chemical endorphins which reinforces the positivity throughout your entire body. Hopefully, you can silence the voices which tell you that it is miserable in the rain. Rain is no bad thing, rain gives life!

A CHOIR IN YOUR DAILY CHALLENGES

The well-known mental trainer, Paul McKenna, described during a lecture how you can overcome your negative thoughts and strengthen your self-confidence in specific circumstances. His trick was to imagine that you have a choir in your head, singing for you when you need strengthening. What type of choir is up to you. Personally, I have a huge gospel choir which sings for me when I need an extra lift. I chose gospel music because I think it is catchy, and full of positivity. The next step is to add background music and special effects. In your mind, you can hire Steven Spielberg to create all the effects that you want.

To give an example of how you can use your inner choir, imagine the following situation: You are approaching a stranger who you find attractive, and you are nervous about talking to him or her. Instead of listening to negative thoughts such as: "He or she is never going to like me, who am I to even think he or she even cares about me?", replace your thoughts with a choir that sings to you. I promise, you will notice an enormous difference. Imagine standing there, hesitating, not knowing if you even dare – and then the choir starts singing: "He's going to walk up to the girl, she's going to be glad that he came and spoke to her".

As a small challenge before you move on to the next chapter, I want you to place yourself in a situation where you know you will feel unsure or uncertain of yourself. And when the uncomfortable feelings start in your stomach, practice the exercise mentioned above. Imagine a huge choir which begins to sing for you, filling you with energy and self-belief and making it easier to go through with what you earlier thought difficult to do.

HEIGHTENED PERFORMANCE

What do you think that elite athletes think, right before they achieve their personal best in a world championship? Do you think that a high-jumper thinks that he's going to knock down the pole on the first attempt, or about how easily his body will sail through the air and glide over the bar with plenty of room to spare?

In sports psychology, it is said that the inner conversation influences performance. A positive inner conversation is supportive and helpful, whereas a negative inner conversation has a harmful effect on how you perform. Therefore, it is important that you learn to dispel negative thoughts and turn them into positive ones. Use the power of the positive voices to gain strength and the conviction you need to succeed.

How do you do that? Every time you have a negative thought, imagine a large red stop sign, the type you will find at traffic junctions. This symbolises that you shall stop the negative thinking and instead focus on something positive.

THE POWER IN THE WORD "YET"

Your performance is greatly affected from how you think about yourself. To be self-confident and be a creative and high-performing power, it is incredibly important that you think positive thoughts about yourself. There is an excellent little word which can be used when you want to be better at thinking positively of yourself. Every time you have the feeling that you are not where you want to be, or do not have the things you want – use the following technique; place the word yet after a negative meaning. For example: I'm not rich, yet! I don't have someone to love, yet! I can't afford a car, yet! I haven't been successful with my business, yet!

Now try it with your own negative thought that makes you feel inadequate.

Did you notice the power in the word *yet*? The word creates a positive expectation and motivates you to keep working towards your goal. You will no longer see yourself as a victim, instead simply someone who hasn't succeeded, yet!

A MORE SECURE ME

Do you recognise in yourself that you walk in a certain way when you are depressed? Do you walk differently when you are especially happy or proud? Our health is mirrored in how we walk and move and a shortcut to feeling better mentally is to think about your posture. If you want to feel better, you should walk as though you are upbeat and happy, or however you want to feel. You will notice an immediate change in how you feel. It takes just a few seconds. The body and mind are tightly connected, and in the same way that you might hang your head as a result of being sad, you can be uplifted as a result of holding your chin up. Our feelings are driven by how we move. If you want to be more self-secure, start by walking as if you already are. Your brain will believe that you are. A simple but very powerful tool!

If you have poor self-belief, it is time to do something about it now. Rip out or copy the following page and stick it up on the bathroom mirror, or some other prominent place where you often find yourself. Read every sentence out loud to yourself several times each day: morning, noon and night. Remember to use the body language that matches what you are reading and that you want to realise within yourself. You will begin to reprogramme your subconscious to start to realise how good you really are and this helps you to succeed in everything you do! If you, for example, need to tell yourself that you are good enough, add a few more points about this. Even if it means that you have to lie to yourself. Do it anyway. Your subconscious will work to achieve what you tell yourself.

One thing you can try, which can awake many feelings within yourself, is looking at yourself in the mirror. Look deep into your eyes and say: I love you! Repeat it several times and look curiously at yourself and how you react when you say it. To begin with, I couldn't say this to my own reflection, but after a few attempts the words came out and soon it became completely natural to pep myself up in front of the mirror when I needed it before an important meeting or presentation. Which feelings are awakened in you when you read the following affirmations?

- » I am good!
- » I am unique!
- » I am just as clever as everyone else!
- » I am just as good as everyone else!
- » I know just as much as everyone else!
- » I can make miracles happen!
- » I can laugh at people who are sent to try me!
- » I can always teach something to the world around me!
- » The world can teach me something, I am a student of life!
- » I was created to give something to this earth!
- » I can achieve anything I want!
- » I am made for success!
- » I deserve happiness and success!
- » Big things are going to happen to me!

CHAPTER 8
HAMPERED BY DEFENCE MECHANISMS

The subconscious is the part of your brain that controls your breathing, heartbeat and other automatic functions. It also drives all your feelings and body movements and thus has a profound influence on your actions. It acts completely upon how it has been programmed, just like a computer. Your consciousness is a very limited part of what we know, and in your subconscious there are often hindrances which prevent you from developing. Our consciousness is sometimes likened to an iceberg where the largest part is submerged beneath the surface.

the conscious
the subconscious

Do you sometimes find excuses for why you do not succeed in certain things? In psychology, it is said that there are defence mechanisms which the subconscious uses to protect us from anxiety and depression. These can also hinder our personal development.

In this chapter, I will explain the most common defence mechanisms and how they, in our subconscious, can act as brake pads in our personal development. Learning to identify these is important in order to be able to pick them up from your subconscious, process them, let them go and begin developing yourself. You will notice that the more you try to avoid these defence mechanisms, the more you will use them and thus hinder yourself in your development. It is suggested that you use the result of using defence mechanisms as a basis for avoiding them in the future. The times that you do use them, it should be used as an opportunity for reflection and development. This way they will gradually be used less often.

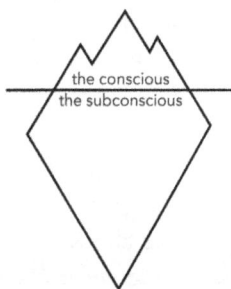

DENIAL

Not so long ago, I saw an advertisement about drug addiction. It said: "If you admit your addiction, there is a way out". In other words, the message was that if you deny your addiction, there is *no* way out. This is exactly what the first defence mechanism is all about, denying that something is going on, or that something has happened.

If you question an addict about his addiction, the answer is often: "I'm not an addict, I can stop whenever I want to". "Why don't you then?" is my response. Regardless of the kind of addiction, it is common to deny it.

Sometimes people react with denial when they are given the message that someone close to them has died. If they do not admit it, they can continue to believe that it has not happened, in order not to have to deal with the grief. The same thing goes for routine visits to the doctor. Many people choose not to go to the appointment, in the belief that they will avoid getting sick. Once they go, it is often too late.

When did you last deny something?

PROJECTION

The next defence mechanism is *projection* or *projecting*. This is when we try to pass a feeling onto someone else which is, in fact, about ourselves. We see our own problems or shortcomings in others. By passing on your problems onto others, you believe you are still faultless. Projection is a common reason for bullying and hatred towards others. Subconsciously you pass over one of your own personality traits, which you have but cannot consciously accept, to somebody else. This way, you distance yourself and take a step back from your own impulses.

A common example are people who reach some type of success. There are always other people who will start to dislike the person who is successful. The person who has worked hard for his success has probably not changed a great deal but grown into the success. The person who is watching with jealousy, may then feel a failure which will manifest itself through dislike for the other person instead. When we project by condemning and rating others, it is a message to ourselves.

When did you last project your thoughts and values onto another person when you were unhappy with yourself?

REGRESSION

Regression means going back to an earlier stage of development. The reason for doing this can be that you are under a significant amount of mental pressure. The body protects itself by going back to an earlier, more carefree state of life which means you can behave more immaturely. This is a way for the subconscious to deal with life's challenges and difficulties. It is not uncommon for students to regress to a less troublesome state of life prior to an exam so they will not have to worry about the exam. Rather they will clean their apartment, exercise or go partying.

When did you last regress? Did you respond to a complaint by becoming childish and putting the blame on someone else instead of taking the responsibility?

INTELLECTUALISING

Intellectualising is yet another interesting defence mechanisms often used for a positive reason, but sometimes can be "misused". Intellectualising means isolating feelings from the intellect in a certain situation. Looking at it matter-of-factly and not letting emotions affect you.

Many see it as a great step forward in their self-development when they have managed to intellectualise in a stressful situation, instead of reacting upon impulse or by reflex. The risk is that you will use this defence mechanism too much, not taking into account other people's views and actions. It will become something that happened, but was not felt.

An extreme example of this is in the Second World War, when the Nazis called the Jews "Untermenschen". This became a way of playing down the execution of women and children. By giving them a name with a lower value than other human beings, it became easier to deal with the violence. When they later started to think about what they had done, many soldiers were hit by extreme depression and anxiety. Have you ever intellectualised? How was your behaviour received by others?

RATIONALISING

A very common form of defence mechanism is that of *rationalising*. Rationalising means that you reconstruct reality, following a situation. An example is the couple who wanted to buy a house. They had been to the viewing and dreamt about how they would renovate and furnish it. When they eventually lost the bidding, they began to rationalise: "We wouldn't have been able to afford it, it was too big for us, there were far too many rooms to clean and heat, it is probably for the best…"

It is said that the more intelligent and creative a person is, the more likely it is that he or she is good at rationalising. By rationalising you lie to yourself, thus blocking the possibility for development and change. A creative person often finds it easier to find arguments for the rationalising to be true. They will quickly come up with several reasons for them not to achieve their goals.

When did you last rationalise?

SHIFTING

Have you ever been reprieved by, for example, your boss, only to notice that you are a little more irritated at your partner when you get home? Then you may have subconsciously used the defence mechanism of *shifting*. Shifting means transferring a behaviour, interest or urge from its prime objective to another one, because the prime is associated with too much anxiety. Instead of dealing with the problem directly with your boss, it is easier to shift your anger onto someone closer to you.

If you have small children, you may recognise yourself in the example where you are getting ready to go out and you are running late. The children won't listen and they won't dress themselves. In this situation, it is easy to take out your own stress and frustration on the children and you will be unreasonably angry with them for not doing what you want them to do.

When did you last shift a problem onto someone else?

SELECTIVE PERCEPTION

Have you ever been in the process of renovating your home, and considered hiring a carpenter? Have you noticed how you suddenly see advertisements for carpenters everywhere? You come across carpenters' vans whenever you are out in the traffic, and they are parked neatly on your neighbours' drives. Do you think this is because many more carpentry businesses have suddenly started? No, there were probably just as many carpenters before, but earlier your brain filtered this away, as it was of no interest to you at the time. This is called *selective perception*. The brain filters away everything that is of no interest, just focusing on what is useful at the time.

One example of how to manage how the brain filters, is the story of the boy who was asked to go to the kitchen to fetch the salt for his father. The boy said: "I don't know where it is, I won't be able to find it". Eventually, he went to the kitchen and, having looked for the salt for a few minutes, shouted: "I can't find it!". When his father came into the kitchen, the salt was there right in front of the boy but without him being able to see it.

You can tell yourself that something isn't there, and you can look and look, even though it is right in front of you. This has happened to me several times, for example when I have been searching for an important document. I have looked all over for it in the piles of paper without finding it. Finally, I have asked someone to help me, and they have found it straight away on the top of the pile right in front of my eyes.

In the same way, you can tell yourself that you are unable to solve a problem. If you tell your subconscious that you can't solve a problem, it will prepare itself for you not to succeed. Your brain will filter away the solutions to your problem. If you instead turn it around and tell yourself that you *can* solve the problem in front of you, your brain will start to find solutions and will present them to you. You will then see possibilities and solutions that you otherwise would not have seen.

CHAPTER 9
WHO ARE YOU, REALLY?

Knowing others is wisdom, knowing yourself is enlightenment. He who controls others may be powerful, but he who has mastered himself is mightier still.
– Lao Tzu

I often wonder why people act the way they do, why they get irritated or happy about things that I say or do. I never used to understand why something I said made one person act in one way, but another person act completely differently. Then one day, I was introduced to a tool which helped me understand why people act the way they do. It is a personality test called IDI (Interpersonal Dynamic Inventory), where you and people around you answer questions about how you are and how you are perceived.

The test measures three "dimensions", and from these dimensions, four different personality types are created with a description of how adaptable you appear to be as a person. You could say that IDI gives you feedback on how your behaviour is perceived by other people. From the description I give in this chapter, you will receive an opportunity for heightened self-insight by scrutinising yourself in different situations. By working with yourself in this way, you can become better at understanding your own behaviour, understanding others and adapting your behaviour depending upon the people around you. As a leader, you will be able to get better at making your co-workers feel validated, according to who they really are, and you will achieve completely new results within your organisation.

As a leader, you will benefit from introducing this way of thinking to your co-workers. By performing this or similar personality tests in your group, and then looking at each other's result with a humble approach, can lead to a considerably more harmonious and contented place of work where the strength of each individual is used to best effect. From the insights, you will start to put each other's strength and weaknesses into situations which have or will occur and you will gain an understanding of how different personalities affect your results.

Having come across many different models trying to explain human behaviour, I have become hooked on the IDI model. I have discovered that it is easy to learn and it is very good to use when I meet people, both privately and as a member of a group. When you start to understand the model and how your fellow human beings act in different situations, the number of small conflicts in your daily life will reduce significantly. The model has helped me to realise my strengths and weaknesses, which I now think about daily to make me a better leader and human being. I have also become better at adapting to other peoples' behaviours in order to create better relationships.

The model is based upon four basic behaviour types and it is important to remember that no type is better than another. To know exactly what behaviour type you have, it is recommended to conduct a test which is available on the market. However, I have noticed that knowing the model and having a good degree of self-insight can give a good start. In any case, it has worked wonders for me. I have achieved a much better relationship with my wife, colleagues and friends, just by taking in the theory connected to the model and understanding the differences between people. Now I want to give you the chance to better your relationships with your work colleagues and the people close to you.

THE IDI MODEL

The IDI model consists of a matrix with a horizontal and vertical line.

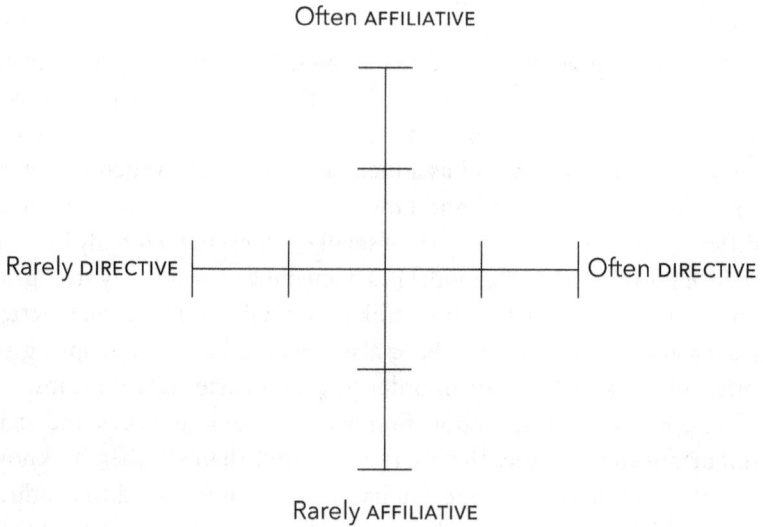

Often AFFILIATIVE

Rarely DIRECTIVE ⊢——————⊦——————Often DIRECTIVE

Rarely AFFILIATIVE

The IDI matrix

The horizontal dimension is called "directiveness", and measures how often a person is perceived to strive to impress, influence and control other people and the world around them. On the left side of the line is the person who is rarely directive. A typical description of such a person is that he is humble, low-key, easy-going, traditional, non-confrontational, quiet, slow. To the right we have the person who is often directive and described as audacious, bold, ambitious, competitive, loud, self-assured, risk-taking and a leader.

The vertical dimension is called "affiliation", and it measures how often a person is perceived to strive to establish an emotional contact with other people. On the upper part of the line is the person who is often affiliative. This person has traits such as accessible, easy-going, hot-headed, informal, nonchalant, restless, emotional, undisciplined and disorganised. On the lower part of the line is the person who is rarely affiliative. Such a person is often perceived as formal, serious, introverted, disciplined, cold, mature, objective, impersonal, organised, structured, a thinker and a loner.

Together, these two dimensions make up the IDI matrix. The dimensions are completely independent of one another and by crossing them, they make up four basic behaviour types.

Based upon what we have already discussed, where do you think you belong?

FOUR BASIC BEHAVIOUR TYPES

There are four basic behaviour types in the model. These are *relator, motivator, producer* and *processor*, and we will now look closer at each style.

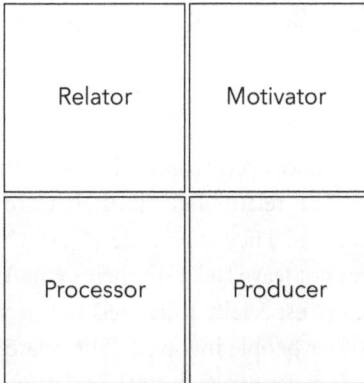

Relator	Motivator
Processor	Producer

The basic behaviour types of the IDI model.

RELATOR

The first type is called *relator*.

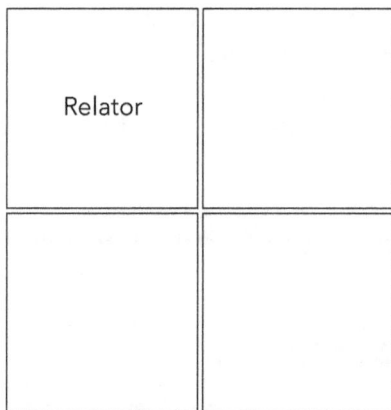

Relator in the IDI model

A relator is perceived as warm and friendly with an easy-going, cooperative manner and a strong need for close personal relationships with other people.

In General:
A relator is a willing and loyal co-worker that performs his work quietly without complaints. The relator likes jobs that are stable and have a strong human connection. They appreciate a boss who takes the time to talk to them and does not leave them on their own. A relator approaches change with great care, especially if he feels that it will affect the relationships with the other people involved. The relator is often scared of conflict, since he does not want to lose the relationship he has or is in the process of building.

As a leader, the relator is careful in his actions and spends a lot of time with his co-workers, in order for everyone to have a part in the decision that he has reached. The need to be appreciated by his co-workers often makes it difficult for a relator to have a confrontation when needed.

Body Language:
The body language of the relator is relaxed and there is often a desire for eye contact. Their eyes are warm and friendly.

Verbal Communication:
During verbal communication, they often use softer and less definitive words such as: if, maybe and possibly. They often talk about particular people and they show clearly that they are interested in relationships with other people. When answering questions, the answers tend to be careful and sometimes disconnected. The relator is careful of saying something that may hurt others.

Written Communication:
Written communication from a relator is usually warm and personal. The relator writes with feeling and openness and tends to write in a long-winded and "talkative" way.

Perception of Time:
The relator's view of time is that it is there for social interactions. It is not uncommon for a relator to be late because of an unwillingness to leave somebody else.

Driving Force:
The relator is motivated by being liked, and they want to be told they are liked.

MOTIVATOR

The next basic behaviour type is the *motivator*.

Motivator in the IDI model

A motivator is perceived as enthusiastic, engaging and exciting. He likes to be with other people, especially if he has the chance to be the centre of attention.

In General:
A motivator is a creative dreamer with an optimistic view of life, which means he will often take personal and professional risks which his more level-headed work colleagues will avoid. The motivator normally has many irons in the fire. If the motivator loses interest in a job, he quickly lets go and find something else that flicks his switch. The motivator blooms when he is appreciated and receives acknowledgement, and will gladly take on work that gives him the attention he needs. The motivator prefers situations that are informal and he finds it easy to show his feelings and be very open, which can frighten people who are not used to it.

As a leader, the motivator has a great ability to lift ideas and sell them to bosses, co-workers and others. Some can find the motivator to be overwhelming and that he can hinder the creativity and independence of others since he, himself, often takes up a lot of space.

Body Language:
A relaxed motivator tends to sit as though the chair was a part of him. The motivator uses an open posture and often finds it hard to sit still. The eyes are warm and move from person to person. Gestures are big, wide and open, with many lively facial expressions and body movements.

Verbal Communication:
A motivator likes to use me-orientated, positive words such as: I believe, I think and I feel. The content is normally about himself. The motivator answers questions very quickly and tends to think out loud. The answers are often perceived as disconnected with many side-tracks and the motivator often fails completely to answer the question itself.

Written Communication:
Written communication from a motivator is usually long and unconnected. The motivator is creative in his written style, particularly if he wants to persuade and enthuse the reader. Written text often includes lively descriptions and humour. It can be difficult to read into exactly what it is the motivator is trying to say, especially because he often finds difficulty in sticking to the point.

Perception of Time:
A motivator often talks about the future. The purpose of time is to be enjoyed, and he often appears to have little respect for time and its use. The motivator uses his, and other people's, time unwisely with unrealistic and irrelevant activity.

Driving Force:
To be unique, especially in being appreciated by many people at the same time.

PRODUCER

The next behaviour type in the model is the *producer*.

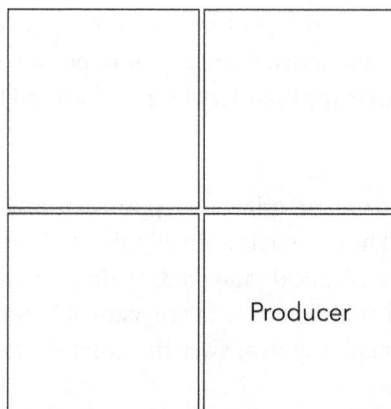

Producer in the IDI model

A producer is perceived as independent, full of initiative, ambitious and competitive. The producer places great value in performance, especially his own.

In General:
A producer is quick to analyse a situation, identify current possibilities and acts on them. In demanding situations, the producer takes responsibility through determining which goals and means are necessary to perform the task. Whilst working, the producer may act authoritatively if his position or decisions are challenged. The producer strives for authority and responsibility and his performance is often seen as a threat to others. The producer easily becomes so engulfed in pursuing his own agenda, that he rarely sees the needs of others around him.

As a leader, the producer prefers to be up-to-date in all details and to be the one who brings others towards the goal. He has difficulty in delegating power and responsibility to others. The producer tends to act from a position of authority and power which can lead his co-workers to the conclusion that the task is more important than the people carrying it out. The producer's greatest reward is knowing that he has completed a task quicker and better than others would have been able to.

Body Language:
A relaxed producer usually sits forward in his chair with the body stiff and on-guard. The eyes are usually straight, penetrating and challenging. The producer often uses fast, brisk and powerful gestures.

Verbal communication:
A producer likes to use strong words such as: must, should and this is how it is… Communication content concentrates on the task or topic. The producer often answers questions quickly and concisely and usually with a straight answer.

Written Communication:
Written communication from a producer is usually short, concise and to the point. It contains little or no action alternatives and is often carefully written. The information provided relates to the topic and nothing more.

Perception of Time:
A producer often talks about the here and now. Time is for doing things. The producer tends to fill all available time with productive activity which gives concrete results. He is often punctual and thinks badly of people who are not.

Driving Force:
To have influence and power, especially in the form of greater and more important tasks.

PROCESSOR

The next basic behaviour type in the IDI model is the *processor*.

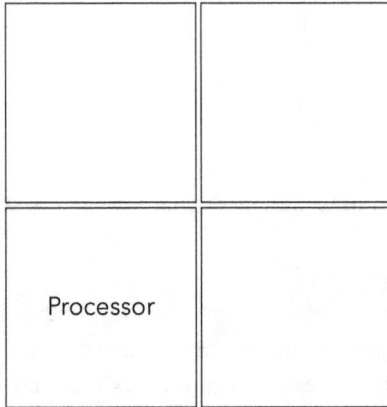

Processor in the IDI model

The processor is perceived as logical, analytical and factual with a great need for structure, safety and order.

In General:
The processor feels safe when all facts are available for the right decision to be made. The processor works best if he has enough time to carefully consider all the alternatives. The processor's need for well thought out, safe decisions means that he is often prone to over-analysing. As a leader, the processor has a strong ability to structure and solve complex problems. He tends not to pay much attention to human relations.

Because of the processor's need for accuracy, he answers questions in a technical way which is often more complex and detailed than needed. The processor is satisfied when he knows that the analysis or plan is well executed, sometimes independently of the result. It can be more important how the processor reaches the result than whether the result is successful.

Body Language:
Even when the processor is relaxed, he tends to sit quite far back on his chair with his body rather closed, stiff and unmoving. His eyes are often unfocussed, as if trying to find the answer, and the processor rarely makes direct eye contact.

Verbal Communication:
The processor uses many questioning words such as: But what if, don't you think, and isn't the case... The content is about how, in other words the method, and he tends to answer questions slowly so he has time to think and formulate the answer. The answer often contains alternatives and suggestions and is seen normally to be well thought-out, exact and carefully formulated.

Written Communication:
Written communications from a processor tends to contain factual or matter-of-fact information, technical data or specific concise questions. The communication is often reserved and rarely contains feelings or emotional reactions.

Perception of Time:
A processor often weaves together the here and now and the future. Time is a valuable resource to be protected. He tends to use time in a rational and well-planned way and usually for logical reasoning.

Driving Force:
The driving force for the processor is being respected for his competence.

SUB-TYPES

Each of the four types we have discussed; relator, motivator, producer and processor, have four "sub-types".

A-1 Friendly Relator	B-1 Expressive Relator	C-1 Friendly Motivator	D-1 Expressive Motivator
A-2 Analytical Relator	B-2 Forceful Relator	C-2 Analytical Motivator	D-2 Forceful Motivator
A-3 Friendly Processor	B-3 Expressive Processor	C-3 Friendly Producer	D-3 Expressive Producer
A-4 Analytical Processor	B-4 Forceful Processor	C-4 Analytical Producer	D-4 Forceful Producer

Sub-types of the IDI model

The sub-types are constructed in the same way as the main types. In other words, a relator can be one of four combinations: relator-relator, relator-processor, relator-motivator, and relator-producer. If you do not fully recognise yourself as one of the basic behaviour types, it is possible that you have one of the other three behaviour types as a sub-type.

Here is an example:

C-3 Friendly Producer	D-3 Expressive Producer
C-4 Analytical Producer	D-4 Forceful Producer

Sub-type producer

Let us say that you are a producer but you also like to sit down and reflect. This will probably put you in the c4 box – an analytical producer – which means that you are a producer but with some traits of a processor. This is especially obvious if you spend time with others who are also producers. Then it will be easier to see what sub-type you are.

Learn to identify what types your loved ones are and, if possible, which sub-types they are. This way, you will be able to interact with them in a way that works better for them and your relationship will improve.

ADAPTING YOUR OWN TYPE

By adapting yourself according to who you communicate with, you can avoid many unnecessary conflicts and, as a boss and leader, you can get more out of your employees.

If you perform the IDI test, it can measure how good you are, as a person and leader, at adapting to the people performing the test together with you, about you. It is measured in a third dimension called "adaptability". It measures how much you are perceived to change certain parts of your basic behaviour type in the short-term, based upon your willingness to cater to the needs of other people in different situations. In other words, your adaptability is perishable and cannot be measured long-term but is completely steered by your willingness to be flexible to different extents in different situations.

Adaptability is measured on a scale from low to high. A person with low adaptability is described as stable, limited, predictable, inflexible, unchanging, rigid, unmalleable and single-minded.

A person with high adaptability is described as flexible, malleable, inconsistent, unpredictable, varied, adaptable, a chameleon and situational.

How much do you adapt your type towards the person you are communicating with and those you are leading?

How high an adaptability should a leader have? According to research, there is a connection between high levels of adaptability and success. There is a top level, somewhere between 65 and 95 percent, which means a very high level of adaptability. But beware, if you have more than 95 percent adaptability, there is a high risk that you will be perceived as less effective and people will find it difficult to know where you stand. In other words, people consider that you blow with the wind or change colours like a chameleon. There is a test where you can determine your exact level of adaptability, but we can still get an approximate picture of how much you should adapt as a leader.

Ask yourself the following questions:

» What is my behaviour type?

» What are the behaviour types of my loved ones?

» What are the behaviour types of my work colleagues?

» What problems have my ignorance of personality types led to in the past?

INTERACTING WITH THE DIFFERENT BEHAVIOUR TYPES

To learn to positively lead and socialise with the different behaviour types, you must first find out which types you will meet. Then you need to find out what motivates the different types and the main behaviours they possess.

As I said before, a relator is motivated by being appreciated and liked. Therefore, you should show extra gratitude for a job well done, when communicating with a relator. A relator enjoys being in a relaxed, informal environment, so avoid acting authoritatively when asking a relator for help. You should also remember that a relator would rather avoid conflict than solve it. Therefore, it is important that you ask questions in the correct way and raise their concerns if there appears to be something beneath the surface disrupting the work or the relationship.

A motivator's driving force is being unique and the centre of attention. He enjoys being given extra space, for example during meetings, where he can publicly present the task he has been given to perform. If you want to make a motivator feel good, be generous in enforcing his feeling of uniqueness and competence in front of others. Make sure to create a stimulating environment with plenty of challenges for the motivator. Use the motivator if you need someone to enthuse and stimulate your work colleagues when you introduce new routines or need to ask them to work overtime.

A producer likes to feel influential and in control. They are motivated by performing their work faster and better than others, feed this need in them. Give the producer a task to solve with a clearly defined goal – he will solve it. The producer enjoys a work environment where things happen, and where demands are put upon them. The producer gets irritated when things come to a standstill and if decisiveness in the group is lacking.

A processor is motivated by being acknowledged for his competence. Praise him for this and ask for precise facts when you are reasoning, so that he gets a chance to show how much he knows. The processor will be able to give you these facts with great detail if you have the time to listen. He prefers a work environment which is stable and structured and he does not like surprises, which means that he should be given plenty of time before possible changes occur.

BEHAVIOUR TYPES IN CLOSE RELATIONSHIPS

IDI is not only a tool used in organisational leadership. The different personalities are everywhere in society. In the queue at the supermarket, at the football game and at the hairdressers. The insight in this model has been most useful to me in my relationship with my wife and with my family and friends. My wife is a relator and I am a producer, in other words complete opposites according to IDI. This can obviously lead to many conflicts if you are not aware of or do not understand the differences between you. We have noticed that, through the insight in this model and the strengths and weaknesses in one another's behaviour type, we have gained a much wider understanding for why the other thinks and acts as they do in different situations. We have also become better at adapting our own type according to the other person in the relationship, and using each other's strengths. I think this is important in order to live in a happy and developing relationship for the rest of our lives.

DIFFERENT LEVELS OF YOUR IDI MATURITY

As I have mentioned, IDI is a useful tool in understanding other people and getting to know yourself better. But there is a danger in categorising yourself in a certain behaviour type. Your weaknesses can start to be used as an excuse for your actions which is, of course, never acceptable. Therefore, I want to emphasise the importance of you practising adapting according to who you are leading or living together with.

Below is a list describing your personal maturity when it comes to the IDI model and leading other people. I have created the list based on my own experiences.

1. The first level of maturity is learning how to identify which basic behaviour type you are, your strengths and your weaknesses, and deciding to actively work with them.

2. The next level of maturity is learning how to identify the basic behaviour types of the people you are leading and living with. Your friends, colleagues and loved ones.

3. The highest level of maturity is starting to adapt your own basic behaviour type to those you are working or socialising with. You are using the knowledge you now possess about how different behaviour types work. You strive to find the optimum level of adaptability according to every individual in order to create a strong relationship.

The highest level of maturity can be referred to as situation-adapted leadership, where the situation and the person you are leading will determine how he or she will be led. When you reach this level, it means that the old saying "treat others as you would be treated yourself" no longer applies. Instead, you will be living according to the saying "treat others as they want to be treated". By approaching other people according to how they want to be treated, it will become easier to maintain a relationship with them at work and in your spare time, and their motivation will increase. Bear in mind that you can never get other people to adapt their behaviour towards you, the only thing you can change is yourself.

BEHAVIOUR TYPES AS ANIMALS

To make it easier and more fun to understand the different personality types, you can draw likenesses to animals.

The relator can be likened to a dog because they like company and they want to be appreciated when they do something good.

The motivator can be likened to a crocodile because crocodiles have big mouths and small ears. They talk more than they listen.

A producer can be likened to a rhinoceros. Once they start running, it can take a long time for them to change direction if someone or something tries to influence them.

A processor can be likened to an owl. It sits on its branch and discovers a rat. It calculates exactly how to fly to catch it. It flies down, takes the rat and flies back to its branch.

If you want to learn more about IDI or see a list of who in the UK are licenced practitioners and can help you with the test, visit www.idiuk. co.uk/

CHAPTER 10
GROUP DEVELOPMENT

In the US Navy, the officers noticed that the groups of sailors on the different ships were very diverse in their efficiency despite having the same tasks, equal qualifications and similar experience. This puzzled them so much that they eventually conducted an inquiry. A scientist by the name of Will Schutz was given the task of studying the different groups of sailors. The result of his research led to a group development model called FIRO, Fundamental Interpersonal Relations Orientation. The model has since been further developed by several researchers, but the basic thoughts are the same.

This chapter will be completely dedicated to the development of groups and what happens in various stages in the group, and how this affects your leadership. You are probably a member of many diverse groups: at work, through spare time interests and with you family. A group can consist of as few as two people and, if you have an earlier relationship with somebody within a larger group, you will also have your own group process.

To understand what happens in a newly-created group, how it develops and how it can best be led through its entire development, I will use a model called FIRO. This model is used both in the Swedish Defence Force and in civilian leadership. The model divides the group development into different phases based on the group maturity. It helps us to understand how leadership should be adapted to the different levels of maturity of the group.

Regardless of whether you are a leader of a group or a group member, the FIRO model will be of some use to you. If you are a leader, you will gain better understanding of what happens in the group and how to lead it. If you do not have any formal leader role in the group, this model will teach you how to understand what you and your colleagues are going through. You will learn how to sense when the group is entering a role-searching phase and you will become aware of the relief when the group moves on in its development and the roles have been filled. By having the knowledge of what happens to you and your colleagues, your understanding of how the group and its members act will increase.

THE FIRO MODEL

The model comprises three main phases and two transitional phases.

Main Phases:
  » Inclusion
  » Control
  » Openness

Transitional Phases:
  » Conviviality
  » Idyll

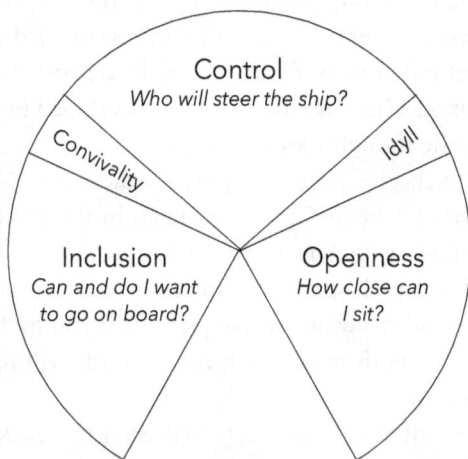

The FIRO model

The Inclusion Phase
For the new group and its members, the first phase is about whether they want to, and are allowed, to join the new group.

Common questions the group members ask themselves:
  » Do I fit into this group?

» Who else is in the group?

» Do I want to join them?

» Am I allowed to join them?

Common behaviour in the group:
» Talking too much or being overly open.

» Some people may pull away or be quiet.

» Checking the eligibility and competences of the other members.

» Telling "tall tales".

» Checking the leader's eligibility and competences.

» Questioning the group's goals and norms.

In the inclusion phase, members try to get to know one another. They question their own and other people's values, are very polite to one another, create little conflict and try to read and interpret non-verbal and symbolic signals.

The group demands order and structure and shows a strong reliance on the leader. As a leader, it is important to give the newly-formed group structure, to create order and to be clear upon which rules apply if you are to be a member of the group.

In a loving relationship, this is a phase where we normally experience the first feelings of love and we float around in the clouds. A similar feeling can be experienced when we join a new club or start a new class. When we get to the inclusion phase, we find it so much fun with all the new people and our experience is that everyone is very kind to you and to each other.

The Conviviality Phase
The conviviality phase is the transitional phase between the belonging and role-searching phases. The group members develop a feeling of "we

are all in it together" and they demonstrate more openly their level of engagement in the group.

The group will enter this transitional phase only once everybody has felt their membership and really feel they are a part of the group. It is always the last person that determines the development of the group. It means that as long as one or more people have not joined the group fully, the group cannot move to the next phase.

During the inclusion phase, all conflict is avoided as much as possible since it is often hard to deal with the question of power and responsibility in a completely new group.

Control Phase

The next main phase is the control phase, also known as role-searching phase or the conflict phase. In the control phase, all focus and energy is directed towards the question of who shall lead the group. One or more people within the group tries to lead or give direction for the group's activities. For the group to enter the control phase, it has to be given a task which requires somebody to take on the role of leader, or for the group to compare competences and abilities amongst the members and together select a leader.

Typical characteristics amongst members in this phase:

» Creating sub-groups and showing less group spirit.

» Showing more open competitiveness between one another and between sub-groups.

» Trying to persuade the other group members about which views are the right ones.

» Showing a refusal to be affected by others.

» Growing frequency and intensity of conflicts.

» Trying to take or avoid leadership with the help of others.

» Trying to solve conflicts by voting, compromising or with outside help.

- » Actively trying to expose other people's "hidden motives" but are very careful about not revealing their own.

- » Giving each other feedback which is often fierce and hostile.

- » Showing a great need for structure and leadership but being unwilling to allow others in the group to fulfil this need.

- » Conduct a revolt against the formal leader.

- » Choosing the oldest or least influential member to be the leader.

- » Carry out a vote when selecting a leader.

As a leader, you should give the group tasks to solve on their own, and you are only to steer when needed. In the control phase, the group is at its most inefficient, and very little will be produced by the group.

If you are in a relationship, this is a sensitive period. This is where the roles are being filled within the family: who is going to lead and who is going to be the one to follow. I believe that many relationships founder during this phase, as they lack insight into how a family, as a group, develops. However, I do believe that the role of leader in a couple's relationship or in a family is not the leader of everything, but rather it is about who takes on the leadership in certain areas in the home. Someone becomes the leader in washing clothes, and someone will be the leader in washing the car, for example.

Idyll Phase
The next transitional phase in the model is called the idyll phase. The idyll phase comes after the control phase where normally there has been an intense conflict between members of the group. The result of these conflicts is that the group now feels liberated. This feeling is hard to understand if you have not experienced it yourself. It is a great feeling of relief after an intense period and the feeling is similar to being in love.

Openness Phase
The last phase of the model is called the openness phase and this is the phase at which the group performs at its best.

Many groups never reach openness in their group development. To reach the openness that characterises this phase, a developed leadership is needed both within the group and the organisation within which they are working.

Typical characteristics amongst the group members are:

» Dealing with conflict as it arises.

» Showing synergy, i.e. they have discovered that working together within the group often achieves better results than individual work.

» Demanding that solutions have been agreed together.

» Openly sharing each other's feelings, views and feedback.

» Showing they are pleased with their role in the group and the group's activities.

» Showing a feeling of "we are invincible".

» Putting other groups down: "they are not as good as we are".

» Defending the group, both internally and externally.

» Making high demands on group loyalty.

» Sometimes being more playful than interested in their tasks.

The members see conflict as a joint problem which provides them with an opportunity to develop. They feel safe since everyone knows that they are appreciated within the group. They communicate with one another directly, openly, honestly and spontaneously.

Your leadership within the group should be as a mentor. You should be in the background should the group need to ask something. However, you need to keep a close eye on the group to ensure it works as it should and that nothing happens that should not.

When the loving couple has come to this openness phase, they are open and honest with each other. They solve conflicts directly instead of letting irritation build up which later leads to even bigger conflicts. The relationship is now built on trust and they trust each other fully. They constantly strive to make joint decisions about important things that affect the relationship.

THE PHASES AS METAPHORS

I would like to present two metaphors that can be used for you to more easily see the differences in leadership and membership in the different phases.

As a leader:
You are a parent teaching your child to ride a bicycle. In the inclusion phase, you need to use stabilisers and hold the bicycle at all times for the child to feel safe.

In the control phase, the child wants to begin cycling by himself, no longer wanting you to hold the bike. Therefore, you will only hold the bike occasionally when the bike begins to wobble and will then let go again once it is stabilised.

In the openness phase, you know your child can ride his bike and therefore sit at a distance watching him ride his bike around the garden. If you are needed, you are close by, giving support should anything happen.

As a member of a group:
You are standing on a pier in a marina. In front of you is a boat and, in it, a group of people. In the inclusion phase, you need to ask yourself if you want to get on board the boat or not. The group will ask themselves whether or not you should be allowed on board.

In the control phase, you are on the boat and you are all asking the question as to who should steer the boat.

In the openness phase, you ask yourself how close you can sit to the others in the boat, and who you should sit next to.

EFFICIENCY IN THE DIFFERENT PHASES

What are the differences in efficiency in the phases and why? The phase where most things happen, is the openness phase. In this phase, there are no longer conflicts to be solved, so all focus can be directed towards the task which the group must solve together. The phase where the least is achieved is the control phase, since the whole group is searching for a leader at the same time as everybody wants to be independent. This makes cooperation more difficult within the group. In the inclusion phase, a fair amount is achieved and there are no real conflicts. There is an interest and a need to fit into the group and to live up to its expectations, which means that you can sometimes lose focus on the task in hand. At this level, the group has not yet become tight-knit and the potential synergy effects fail to materialise.

CHANGES TO THE GROUP

If someone joins or leaves the group, this will affect the group's maturity. The group will regress back to the first phase in order to start from scratch by creating a sense of inclusion with each other. Unless it is a leader who disappears, formal or informal, the group will more quickly return to the phase they were at before. If a leader leaves the group, it must find a new leader, making the process to bring the group back to the openness phase longer.

Similarly, groups can regress in their development if the group (or couple) have been separated for some time. Have you ever been away from your group or your loved one for a week or a weekend and noticed that you have regressed back to an earlier stage once you meet again? You probably have noticed this, as have I. For a while, it can be a little awkward once you return from, for example, a trip. Why is that? Well, according to Schutz, a group will take a step back in its maturity for a brief period when it is not together. A mature group will recover much quicker than a group which is not as far ahead in its development.

HOLDING BACK A GROUP IN ITS INCLUSION PHASE

There are several examples of companies that deliberately strive to hold back their work groups in the inclusion phase. The airline company SAS is said to do this with its technical staff. This is for several reasons. They want to avoid the group getting into the control phase and thus lose efficiency, and because in the inclusion phase you are still alert and do not fully trust one another. This means that you do not take for granted that somebody else has checked the brakes on the plane – you would rather check it yourself. In order to keep the group in the inclusion phase, they rotate the staff before they have time to move on in their group development.

FIRO-B

FIRO-B is related to the FIRO model and is an individual test you perform as a leader in order to discover which phase of maturity within the FIRO model you strive to lead in. When I performed the test, it showed that I placed much focus on the control phase, which meant that I mainly strived to lead with a steady hand and I did not like to have my role as a leader questioned. However, the test made me think – do I really want to lead in this way? Is it really enjoyable to be led by me when I do it like this? The answers to the questions made me decide to change my style of leadership, and I started to aim for more openness in my leadership. If you are interested in learning more about yourself as a leader of different groups, I strongly recommend you find this test and perform it. The test is available to buy from different companies, but you can also search on the internet for simpler versions which are free, but which still will give a picture of where you are.

Where do you think your focus as a leader lies in the FIRO model?

CHAPTER 11
TO BE A LEADER

A leader is a part of a system that gives energy to the group.
– Unknown electrician

WHAT IS A LEADER?

I would say that a manager is a person who has been formally appointed to make decisions, and a leader is someone who also has the support of his staff. A leader has the support and the will of the group to do something good together. The group feels commitment and participation in working towards the goal.

A leader is a role model who lives according to his expectations of others. It is someone who people look up to and try to emulate. A person who wants the best for the group and does not only look out for himself. The leader ensures he is a step ahead in his knowledge and that he can help others to reach the same level. The leader is unafraid to teach others and does not need to withhold his knowledge as old-fashioned managers may have done. The leader is exactly like the captain of a football team, he brings the team together and ensures they are all aiming for the same goal. Instead of having a bunch of individuals on the football pitch, he has a team who work together to score many goals and win matches.

WHY DO WE NEED A LEADER?

No group can operate without a leader. If no-one takes the initiative to do something, nothing will be done. Imagine a group of mushroom pickers who have gone astray in the forest – nobody takes the role of leader, everyone just sits down on the ground, hoping that someone will come and find them. Instead of stepping up to the situation and finding out if someone in group has any useful skills, they just sit there.

Without a leader, a group cannot move forward. I have heard of many workplaces which are in this situation. They have removed the formal management and instead have installed a flat organisation where the workgroup jointly takes the initiative and takes decisions together. I do not think this is an effective solution. In one of the cases I have heard of, it was a local municipal department which had made this type of reform. In that case, there will always be a need for the group to refer to its higher management – or even to the taxpayer – before decisions can be made. In such a situation, I am convinced that somebody in the group will – more or less secretly – take an informal role of leader and steer the group. The only difference is that the person is not formally tasked as the group leader. As long as nobody is against it, that person will become accepted as the group's leader.

There have been studies carried out on groups without management or leaders, and it has been noted that it has a clearly negative effect on the performance of the group. A group or department choosing to take away its boss, can mean that the group is in the control phase of the FIRO model, and that it cannot decide on who will be the leader. In this case, they would rather be without a boss, thinking this to be the solution to a better functioning department.

ROTATIONAL LEADERSHIP

The knowledge and models that I would like to share about leadership, I have also used within the Army and, especially, in the recruitment group for which I was the boss and which had the task of recruiting new recruits to the Home Guard. In the group, all those who were interested and had the prerequisites to lead, could be project managers for various recruitment opportunities within the battalion. As a result, we not only had someone who could plan and carry out various activities, we also had seven people who could take over my job if I decided to take a step back. It also meant that we had a very broad range of skills in the group, where almost everyone had been able to cover, and get better at, one another's roles.

Work rotation is not a new concept, but managers do not often rotate their duties. However, it is useful in increasing the group members skills and understanding for each other's tasks. In most cases, people like to be given additional responsibility and this became apparent in the recruitment group for which I was responsible. Those who shouldered the extra responsibility grew significantly in their personal development and were strengthened by the confidence given in them.

In days gone by, it was always the eldest who was appointed leader if there was no-one else chosen from within the group. I often encountered this in the Army when I came across new groups. In most cases when we worked within recruiting or took part in an exercise, I was the youngest Officer on duty, but still held the most responsibility. How was that? I think that a strong will and good leadership can erase the obstacles that come with age and a lack of experience.

It is important for a leader to listen and consider the opinions of those he leads. If you – as a leader – involve the group members, instead of taking full responsibility yourself, you have activated more brains and generated more engagement from the group. Group members are likely to feel more involved in the group's work and, by engaging the whole group, this creates a synergy effect which means that we are now a single brain moving in the same direction.

THE REASON FOR DELEGATING

An important part of leadership is understanding that you have limitations, both in time and competence. If you ask for help, you will have more time to focus on the wider organisation. You need to decide if you will think as a small business owner, or if you will think bigger and build a system which is not dependent upon you doing everything alone. By delegating to an expert tasks which you are not particularly knowledgeable about, the work will be done not only better, but also quicker than if you had done it yourself.

When you start to delegate to your co-workers, you will also spread the responsibility which will, in turn, increase the motivation amongst those you delegate to, if it is done well. It depends upon if you are showing an interest and having the confidence that the person will be able to complete the task effectively.

Within the Swedish Defence Force, authority as an Officer has always been a crucial factor. However, it has become more common to change managers, depending upon the task in hand. If there is a soldier who is particularly good at a task which the group has been given, he is able to take over the role of leader until the task is completed. It is a very clever way of making use of the collective competence.

As a leader, how good are you at passing over control and delegating to others?

GOOD AND BAD DELEGATION

Delegation without control is not delegation, it is dumping
– Bob Harrison

There are two ways of delegating; the right way and the wrong way. The right way is to delegate, the wrong way is to dump. What differentiates them is that when delegating, you – as the boss – retain the responsibility. You feel responsible and remain connected to the person you have delegated to, and you follow-up and support them if they need help. If you dump a task on somebody, you don't really care how it goes as long as it is completed. You have devolved yourself of all responsibility and have passed it over to the person you have dumped onto. As a leader, you should avoid dumping, and always strive to delegate. You are there to support the person's journey to the goal and you help them to develop on the way. By showing that you care for your co-workers, they will stick with you and help to carry the organisation forward.

HANDLING CONFLICT

The first thing you need to understand about conflicts is that they are normal and unavoidable. Conflicts can be enriching, and we can often learn something from them, even if it may not feel that way when we are in the middle of them. By adopting the attitude that conflicts are natural, you can deal with them in an earlier stage instead of allowing them to grow bigger.

There are three ways to get out of a conflict. Either person A wins and person B loses, or person B wins and person A loses, or you strive for a win-win situation where both of you leave the conflict as winners. You will then reach a compromise where both parties meet half way.

In the Swedish Defence Force, it is taught that there are five different techniques for handling conflict:

» We force the other party to obey us using instruments of power.

» The parties meet and work together by trying to see things from one another's point of view. Hopefully this leads to a greater understanding for the other party and, together, we can find a solution.

» We find a compromise where we sacrifice certain things in order to satisfy others.

» We choose to avoid solving the conflict by staying away from whoever the conflict is with. This will not solve the conflict and it is not unusual that the person chooses to leave or find another position.

» Another way to handle conflict is to adapt to the other person and back away from our own views in order to satisfy the other party. This will not solve the conflict either, it will only lessen it and it can raise its head anytime later, perhaps in a completely new way.

FEEDBACK

What are you like as a leader? Do you know what your co-workers really think about you? There is only one way to find out what people think of you; ask them. If you take becoming a good leader seriously, you must be prepared to accept the criticism from those you lead, otherwise you will never improve.

When should you ask for feedback? There are two different situations where I normally ask for feedback. I want spontaneous feedback immediately after having done something. I also like to give people the opportunity to really consider what they think, therefore I usually come back to the event later and ask for feedback again. Our brain needs to be able to sleep on certain things so that it can think through what has happened and – as we have spoken about earlier in the chapter about the IDI model – some people need longer to reflect and therefore do not like to give spontaneous feedback. This must be respected and they must be given the time to reflect.

If you want someone to develop, it is important that you understand the following: praise is more efficient than punishment. According to psychologists, we learn better when a good deed is reinforced rather than only receiving feedback when we have done something badly. Therefore, it is important to give feedback when things work well, thus enforcing this behaviour. When things haven't gone so well, you still need to state the positives from what went badly.

DEALING WITH CHALLENGES AND PEOPLE WITH EXPECTATIONS

Kay Pollak once spoke, in a lecture, of a technique he used when making the Swedish film *As it is in Heaven* in order to create a positive picture of all members of the group. He first took a good photograph of every person. He then started getting up in the morning a few hours before everybody else, and took out the photos. He went through the pile and, for every person, he thought or said something positive. For example: "Lena, you are amazing at your work, especially that time you found that special sweater that gave a lift to the entire scene". The effect this has was that he met his cast and staff every day filled with happiness and gratitude. He was completely focused on how good they were – as humans and at their work.

In my life, I have started to practice a similar technique when I am faced with challenges. I tell myself that everything will be fun and exciting and I think only positive thoughts about the people in the situation. In the beginning, I still felt a little nervous, but now I have started to believe in myself completely when I tell myself that it will be fun, and I get excited about meeting the people in question. An incredibly effective technique for shifting focus to something positive and good.

ADJUSTED TEACHING METHOD

As we spoke about in the chapter about IDI, you must, as a leader, learn to adapt your own leadership and your way of teaching according to the person you are leading. You cannot treat other as you want to be treated, this is passé. Instead, you should treat others as they want to be treated. This provides a more effective leadership and more motivated staff. Another key factor in your leadership is that there are different ways of learning and taking in knowledge. We cannot teach something to all our staff in the same way. We must adapt the way we teach in accordance with the type of learning style they have.

In the Swedish Defence Force, a model is used which puts the way we learn new things into four different learning styles:

Concrete Experience (CE)
Reflective Observation (RO)
Abstract Thinking (AT)
Active Experimentation (AE)

Just as in the IDI model, these styles are characterised by different traits. For you to better get your message across, it is important to understand how your fellow human beings – and those you lead – learn. Strive to involve all four learning styles in your education. If you have a group with the same learning style, you can focus mainly on that style of learning when you are educating.

It is also important to understand how you take in new knowledge yourself, so you can adapt your own learning and become as efficient as possible. If you are interested, you can find people or companies online who work with these types of tests. I hope that the following overview will provide you with a hint of which learning style you recognise yourself in. However, you will probably discover that you will see yourself in several of the styles we discuss. If this is the case, think about whether there is one learning style which is more dominant than the others.

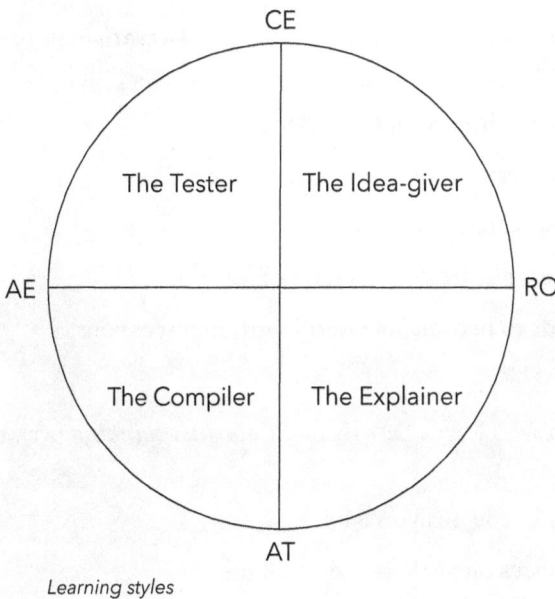

Learning styles

A person who primarily learns through *concrete experiences* (CE), is described as follows:

» Steered by his emotions.

» Is open and experienced-oriented.

» Trusts his emotional experiences.

» Is normally assertive and people-minded.

» Inclined to think that each situation is unique.

» Learns best from exact examples and things that have been experienced.

» Learns the most from discussions with others who have the same learning type.

A person who learns best from *reflective observations* (RO), is described as follows:

» Sees and listens a lot to others.

» Has a testing and objective attitude.

» Trusts careful observations.

» Prefers lectures as a method of learning.

» Tends to become introvert in group discussions.

A person who learns best through *abstract thinking* (AT), is described as follows:

» Thinks and analyses a lot.

» Focusses on analysis and thoughts.

» Trusts in logical thinking and rational processes.

» Is normally more interested in symbols and "things" than in people and emotions.

» Prefers situations which emphasise theories and systematic analysis.

» Often gets disappointed in, and learns little from, unstructured experimental methods.

A person who learns from *active experimentation* (AE), is described as follows:

» Prefers to get things done.

» Is active and action-oriented.

» Trusts experiments.

» Learns best from projects and activities in small groups.

» Does not like passive learning methods, such as lectures.

» Is usually outgoing.

From the answers to the questions in the model, you will fall more or less into one sector and one certain style. The four styles in the model are tester, idea-giver, compiler and explainer.

The Tester:
Gets thingsdone. Creates knowledge from actively doing something. When theory and reality collide, the tester tends to discard the theory.

The Idea-Giver
Is imaginative and creative. Science shows that the idea-giver usually has an abstract imagination and is good at converting knowledge into new situations.

The Explainer
Can generate theoretical ideas and models. He creates models of reality. If theory and reality do not comply, the explainer tends to emphasise the theory.

The Compiler
Is good at formulating and practicing ideas and theories. He turns ideas into practical action based upon logical thought.

As a leader, your task is to make everyone learn as effectively as possible. Not by changing them, but by changing your own way of teaching. In the Swedish Defence Force, they call it experienced-based learning. This is a way of teaching that satisfies all the four styles.

1. Create a concrete experience. This is what CE learns best from.

2. Following the experience, you think it through. What happened? This is what RO learns best from.

3. From the lessons, you create certain generalisations. They are what AT learns best from.

4. When you have completed the generalisations, the group will test these new insights for real. This is what AE learns best from.

The lesson from this, is that you need to broaden your way of educating in order to pass knowledge to others in the best possible way. To satisfy all four learning styles, you must ensure that they are included in all in your lessons or lectures. For a CE-minded person to learn as much as possible, he should be given the opportunity to experience what he is about to learn. If you want to teach an RO-minded person, you should show or tell him what he is about to learn. You need to be theoretical with a AT-minded person and not give all of the solutions at once, let him think a little while for himself. A person who is AE-minded needs to try until he finds his own solution.

CHAPTER 12
TO LEAD YOURSELF OR OTHERS

Earlier, we spoke about personality types and, in this chapter, we will look at a similar model which divides people in how you want to earn money and how much spare time you want. It shows which values dominate your actions when it comes to having an income, and how it affects your leadership.

The basis for this theory is called the Cashflow Quadrant, and it has been described by, amongst others, Robert Kiyosaki. He had an upbringing where two different fathers greatly influenced him. One was his own father – he earned good money and was successful, yet never had time or money left over for his family. The other was the father of his best friend, who also earned good money, but in addition had plenty of time for his family and time to coach and teach Kiyosaki.

The two fathers were very different and supported Kiyosaki in different ways. If you want to learn more about the Cashflow Quadrant, I recommend you read Kiyosaki's book *Rich dad, poor dad*.

CASHFLOW QUADRANT

According to the Cashflow Quadrant, there are four ways to earn money: You can be an *employee, self-employed, business owner* or *investor*.

Employee	Business owner
Self employed	Investor

The Cash Flow Quadrant

I want you to bear in mind that there is no way that is better than the others, they are just diverse ways of earning money which will give different degrees of time left over for other things. Different people are attracted to different sectors of the quadrant. Most of us have the potential to earn money from all four sectors. The way we choose does not depend on what we have learned so far from life, but more on how we are as people and what our basic values are. These values can steer us towards a certain sector.

WHAT ARE THE DIFFERENCES BETWEEN THE DIFFERENT SECTORS?

Some people like to be employed, others hate it. Some people like owning companies, but do not like running them. Others like owning companies and running them. Some like investing whilst others only see the risk of losing money. Below, we shall delve deeper into each way of making money:

Employee:
Those who are employed in companies earn money by working for some-

body else. They work for the money and look for the security of being employed. Creating financial success as an employee takes time, since the income is dependent upon how much you work. The more successful you become, the more time is taken up by work. To raise your income in this sector, you must personally put the time in and work long hours.

Self-employed:
Self-employed people make money by working for themselves in their own companies. They work for money and for the freedom of being their own boss. They want to do their own thing and do not want their income to be dependent upon other people. They want to decide for themselves how much money they should earn. They understand that, unless they work hard, they will not deserve a high salary. They like taking control of a situation and doing something about it.

In this group, there are plenty of specialists who have studied for many years at university, for example doctors and lawyers. Here we also find artists, hairdressers and others. People who are self-employed are usually perfectionists and that is why we choose to use their services. We expect the dentist to be an expert, or that the private doctor will give us the right medicine when we are sick. Many self-employed people find it hard to hire and train other people since they fear that later they will become competitors. For a self-employed person to become a fully-fledged businessman, he needs to turn his knowledge over to a system – which is difficult since they are too attached to their own business.

Business Owner:
The business owner can almost be seen as the opposite of the self-employed person. He owns a company which generates money. He gets tax relief which generates money fast, making the money work for him instead of him working for the money. He looks for freedom in the form of time and money. The business owner likes delegating work to others. His motto is: "Why do the job yourself if you can hire someone else to do it for you, both faster and better?"

A successful business owner can leave his company for a year or two, finding it in a better state than when he left it. He owns a system and hires competent people to run it. To be a successful business owner, you need the ability to lead other people.

Investor:
He earns money through different investments. Money which generates more money. He also gets tax-relief which generates money faster. The money works for him even when he sleeps. The investor looks for both financial freedom and time left over for other things, just like the business owner. This is the sector in which money turns into wealth.

Changing sector means a significant mental change and knowledge of what the target sector is all about. Emotional change is also needed, not just intellectual. If you fail or are afraid of failure in a new sector, there is a risk that you will simply glide back into the original sector you have come from.

Regardless of how much money you earn, you should always put some money into investments to eventually become rich, says Kiyosaki.

IDENTIFYING PEOPLE FROM THE DIFFERENT SECTORS

E: "I'm looking for a decent and safe job with good salary and benefits".

S: "My hourly rate is ... I cannot find the right people to do the job and do it right":

B: "I'm looking for a new MD to run my company":

I: "Is my cashflow based upon an internal gross return or net percentage return?"

By learning to identify which sector a person belongs to, you know what that person strives for and you are able to offer it either as an employer or as an investor. It is also easier to use the right words when talking to the person. Words are powerful. A word that triggers one person can frighten another off. The word "risk", for example, can spark an interest in an investor but can scare someone in the employee sector.

Think about the following questions:
  » Can you grill a better hamburger than McDonalds?
  » Can you build a better system than McDonalds?

If you answer no or don't understand the second question, your focus is probably in the left side E and S. Where do you see yourself and which sector would you like to belong to? If you feel motivated to change sector, it will take self-insight, becoming conscious of your basic values, and being able to change these when needed.

WATER TO THE VILLAGE

To clarify the differences between the left and right sides of the quadrant, I will re-tell a story by Robert Kiyosaki.

There was once a distant village that lacked water. The elders had decided that they needed to get water to the village and had offered it out to contract. There were two people interested; Ed and Bill. The elders in the village decided to give both of them the rights, in order to create some competition and to ensure delivery of water to the village.

Ed immediately bought two stainless steel buckets in order to collect water from the lake a kilometer and a half from the village. He poured the water into the big water tank that the village had built. To be able to deliver the water on-time every morning before the villagers woke up, Ed had to get up very early each morning to carry the water.

Bill, on the other hand, disappeared and wasn't seen for several months, which made Ed happy as he didn't have any competition and earned all the money himself. But instead of running with buckets all day, Bill had written a business plan, started a company, found four investors and hired an MD to do the job. He returned six months later with a team of builders and, within a year, they had installed a water pipe from the lake to the water tank.

At the opening ceremony, Bill announced that his water was cleaner than Ed's since there had been complaints about dirt in Ed's water. Bill also said that he could supply the village with water twenty-four hours per day, seven days per week. Ed could only deliver water during the week since he did not work at weekends. Then Bill announced that, apart from delivering better water quality and a safer supply, he would also charge seventy five percent less than Ed. The village was delighted with Bill's new water pipe.

To compete, Ed reduced his price by seventy five percent, bought another two buckets and new lids to stop the water from getting dirty. He started carrying four buckets every time he went to the lake. To offer a better service, he hired his two sons to help him carry water at night and during the weekends. When his two sons went off to college, he said: "Hurry back, for one day this company will belong to you!" For some reason, his sons never returned when they finished college.

Later, Ed had problems with his staff and with demands from the trade union. They demanded higher salaries and better benefits. The trade union also wanted its members to only carry one bucket at a time. Bill, on the other hand, understood that if this village needed water, there must be more villages with the same requirement. He re-wrote his business plan and then sold his clean, fast, cost-efficient water system to other villages around the world. He does not earn much per bucket but delivers millions of buckets per day. Regardless of whether he is working, millions of people consume millions of buckets of water each day and all that money goes into his bank account. Bill created a water pipe delivering money to him and water to the villages.

Bill lived happily ever after while Ed had financial problems and worked hard for the rest of his life.

Do you recognise yourself in this story? Are you the one who wants to see quick results, running off straight away with the buckets, or do you see the possibility of building a system, a water pipe that works regardless of whether you are there or not? Are you a hard worker or are you a smart worker?

SPEND TIME WITH LIKE-MINDED PEOPLE

There is an American saying that says: "Birds of a feather, flock together. And the flock flies to the same place".

What can we learn from this expression? My interpretation is that we strive towards the same goal as those we spend time with. This means you must examine who you spend time with – what do they want from their lives? If you want to become successful, you should spend your time with people who have already become successful or who strive to become so. If you want to learn the high-jump, you cannot spend time with a discus thrower in the belief you will soon become world champion in the high-jump. You must surround yourself with successful high-jumpers and observe how they do or have done. Then you must emulate them to achieve the same success.

THE MODEL SIMPLIFIED

What do the different styles in the Cashflow Quadrant mean and how can we use them? To simplify the model, you could say that the two styles to the left are for he who wants to do the job himself, and the two styles to the right are for he who would rather see someone else do the job on his behalf. The styles to the right are the ones that earn the most money and have the most time left over for other things.

Kiyosaki says that it is difficult for business owners and investors to explain to employees and self-employed why they do not want a normal job. Every sector has different rules, and different knowledge is needed to be successful in each one.

CHAPTER 13
AN ORGANISATION INDEPENDENT OF YOU

Of course, it is nice to feel needed. It is a widely accepted basic human need. But how does an organisation dependent upon one key person function? It works well as long as that person is there, but what happens if he leaves, gets sick or dies? It probably doesn't work out well and if the person is in a leading role, it will most likely have profound consequences on the organisation.

This chapter is about the benefits of removing the key people from an organisation and turning the whole organisation into the key person. For an organisation to not be dependent upon a single person, it is important that a leader shares out the responsibilities and is prepared for other people to sometime take the lead. Instead of always being the leader, you should find opportunities where it is enough to coach and support those you have delegated responsibility to. You are then no longer dependent upon one person; more people have been exposed to the role and there are now others able to step in and take over when needed. But, bear in mind that this way of working can be difficult to apply to more complex tasks.

ARE YOU THE LEADER OF AN ORGANISATION?

The aim of a leader and business owner should be to free yourself from the organisation. The organisation needs to be able to work without you. This means you will have more time left over for other things. Lecturer Michael Gerber suggests that those running a smaller business should phone their employees and say: "I'm going away for three months!", and then hang up. On the other end of the phone, you will probably hear: "But, but, but, but…". Would you be able to leave your business or position for three months without worrying that the entire organisation will founder?

Going back to the previous chapter about the Cashflow Quadrant, I see a clear connection between leadership type and where you sit in the quadrant. The two styles to the right, business owners and investors, run businesses through others, which means it does not take as much time as it would if they were there managing the daily routine themselves. I would like to remind you that I do not place a value on the different styles – different people enjoy different tasks in life – I would just like to make you think, by asking whether you would like more time to spend with your children growing up, with your favourite sport, or with your friends?

A SMALL ORGANISATION WITH FEW LEADERS

Recently I had lunch with a friend I had not seen in a long time. We talked about his job as a regional manager in a relatively new office of a manpower company. He told me how hard he must work every day and, since his employees are hired out to other companies – he is the one who must take care of all the practical tasks; buy furniture, write advertisements for newspapers, pre-pay salaries, and so on.

He also told me something that fascinated me a great deal. He had delegated some of the responsibilities for the company to his employees in the field. For example, recruiting welders. Since he did not know anything about welding, he felt it appropriate to seek the help of someone who did. In this case, he used a welder employed via his manpower company. The welder had been given the task to, alongside his usual tasks, follow welding courses in the local area and recruit talented welders as they completed their training. Long-term, this way of working will provide some relief to the management so they are able to focus on tasks which will develop the company instead. In businesses where staff are constantly on-site, this is normal practice. Responsibility is shared and everybody does their bit. However, this was the first time I had heard about this way of using the collective competence in a manpower business.

CHAPTER 14
FEEDBACK

Never complain about the things you permit to go on in your life.
  – Mike Murdock

WHAT IS FEEDBACK?

Feedback is a way of improving relationships and performance in a work team, in your family or with your friends. Giving someone feedback is telling them what you think about the way they have acted in a certain situation, both positive and negative. It is down to the recipient of the feedback to decide what they do with the views and influences that it brings.

WHY GIVE FEEDBACK?

Why do you give feedback? I can think of two reasons, where one is about the person you are giving feedback to and the other is about you.

To begin with, you can help somebody grow and develop when suggesting changes. As it is often difficulty to see where you can improve yourself, feedback given in the right way can often lead to personal development for the person receiving it.

The other reason is that if the person's behaviour affects your life in a negative way, you must do something about it. You can never complain about something that you allow to happen in your life. Remember this the next time something bothers you and you are deciding whether to give feedback or not.

WHY RECEIVE FEEDBACK?

At the beginning of this book, I gave the example of the Dead Sea, and that it is dead because no new water is ever added to it. The same thing goes for your personal development and with a business. It is said that an organisation that stops developing shows the first signs of death – a person who stops developing will slowly stagnate. If people around you do not give you feedback, you need to start asking for it if you are to continue developing.

GUIDELINES FOR GIVING FEEDBACK

There are a number of guidelines for giving good feedback:

» Aim your feedback directly at the person or group, do not take diversions. Spreading rumours is not an effective way of influencing anybody, it will only lead to unnecessary conflict.

» The person providing the feedback says: "*I* believe, *I* think," not *we* or *you*. Let others speak for themselves, only speak for yourself and about your own views.

» Only give feedback on the behaviour, not the person, and only say things that the person can changes, for example to speak louder or get to work on time. Telling someone with a lisp to stop lisping is pointless.

» Use feedback as a way of opening channels and improving relationships, not for closing and destroying them.

To have a successful dialogue about what you want to exemplify, you should bear the following in mind.

» The opposite party must want to receive feedback. Ask the question: do you want feedback? It opens up the recipient since he has made an active choice to receive the feedback.

» Be objective and straight to the point, write without judging. Do not use general behaviour in your feedback such as: "You are always so messy!" Instead say: "I have noticed that you haven't put your plates into the dishwasher after eating dinner this last week".

» Give examples of times and situations where something has occurred. To create credibility in your views, you must give concrete examples of occasions when the person has displayed the unwanted behaviour that you want to highlight. To give valuable feedback with correct and concrete facts, you should think beforehand and know what the occasions are. This is important for you to be as specific as possible about which behaviour is good or bad and what needs changing.

» Give feedback at the right time. Be sympathetic to whether the person is open to receive the feedback or not.

» Give the right amount of feedback. If you have lots to say, say a little at a time so that the recipient has time to digest the information before you give more.

» To increase the effect of your feedback, you should use real feelings. A feeling cannot be questioned by others, it is your own. Using feelings in your feedback often leads to people listening and seeking contact with you in order to hear more.

SEPARATING THOUGHTS AND FEELINGS

What is the difference between a thought and a feeling? A feeling is something that you feel within yourself as it happens. Examples of feelings are: anger, sadness, bewilderment, peacefulness, inspiration, happiness and fear. Feelings are your own and nobody can tell you that you are not angry or happy. If you say: "I get sad when you…", it cannot be denied. That is the way you feel. Thoughts are what we think the other person does with or to us. Examples of thoughts are: rejection, cheated, used and appreciated. Thoughts can easily be questioned by the receiver: "You haven't been cheated at all…"

An example of good feedback with feeling is: "I feel inadequate when you do not praise me when I have done something well. It makes me sad inside."

ACTIVE LISTENING

If you are to receive feedback, you need to decide to learn from what the other person has to say. If the other person has chosen to expose his feelings to you, you need to receive the feedback well in order to better the relationship. Here are a few tips for becoming a good listener:

» Clear your head of everything else and concentrate on the message that is being conveyed.

» Decide to have a listening attitude, even if the person is tiresome to listen to or if you think he is wrong.

» Ask questions to ensure that you have understood the messages correctly.

» Adopt a positive attitude for the person giving the feedback and conclude that you will carry the discussion forward so that you can solve the problems raised by the feedback.

» Do not question the other person's feelings.

» Paraphrase so that you can confirm that you have understood correctly. For example: "If I understand you correctly, you mean that I…"

» Don't give advice when you are supposed to be listening.

» Listen instead of thinking about what to say next.

» Remember, it is by listening to others that we can learn something new about ourselves.

THE FEEDBACK STAIRCASE

For feedback to lead to improvement, you must receive it in a positive way. The feedback staircase describes different levels of maturity that we choose when receiving feedback.

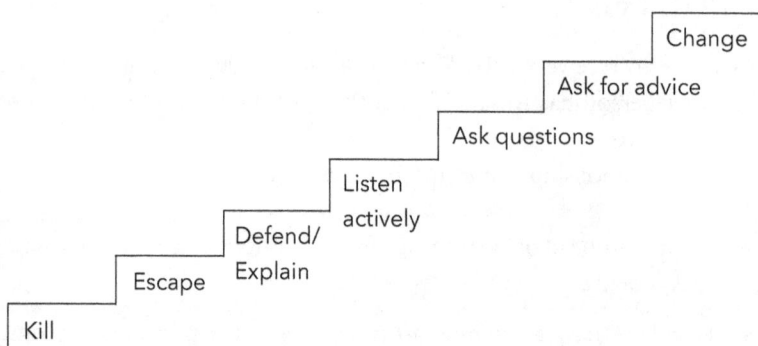

The Feedback Staircase

The feedback staircase shows different steps you must climb to receive feedback in a mature manner and then do something about the opinions people have about you and your actions.

» The first step in to *kill* the feedback. When you receive feedback at this level, you tell the person who is providing it that he is wrong, end of story!

» The next step is to *escape*. This way you avoid talking about the subject that is brought up.

» The third step is to *defend* and *explain*. In this phase, you try to defend your actions and try to explain that what you are doing is right.

» The fourth step is to start to *listen actively*. Here you listen actively to the different points of view and you take it with you and reflect.

» The fifth step is starting to *ask questions*. You are interested to know more and you want to ensure that you have understood correctly so you start to ask questions.

» The sixth step is *asking for advice*. "How can I become better at motivating my co-workers?"

» The last step is actually creating a *change* from the feedback you receive.

THE JOHARI WINDOW

The Johari Window is a psychological model created by Joseph Luft and Harry Ingham which describes how open we are towards others and how much other people know about us, which we do not know ourselves. Here, inner security, trust in others, feedback and openness come together to form a model which can lead to greater insight and development within you as an individual.

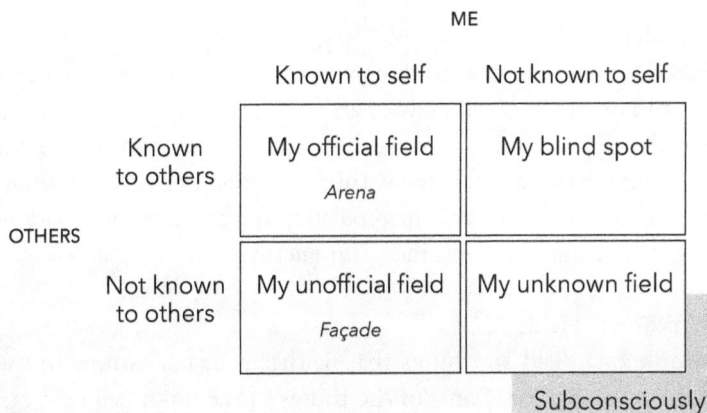

	ME	
	Known to self	Not known to self
Known to others	My official field *Arena*	My blind spot
Not known to others	My unofficial field *Façade*	My unknown field
		Subconsciously

The Johari Window

The model comprises four fields: the arena, the blind spot, the façade and the unknown field.

The Arena:

In the arena field, there exists everything you know about yourself and everything other people know about you. The arena includes all your everyday opinions and behaviours that you show to the world. When trust for an individual or group increases, the size of the arena also increases. A small arena field means that you are not ready to expose yourself very much in front of the group or to share many of your inner feelings. It is not unusual that you choose to reduce your arena when you join a new group, to then gradually increase its size as confidence in the members of the group increases.

The Blind Spot:

The blind spot contains things which you yourself are not aware of but which can be seen by others. It normally consists of unconscious actions such as gestures and facial expressions. To be aware of these actions, you must receive feedback thus making the blind spot smaller.

The Façade:

The façade field consists of everything you know about yourself, but that is unclear to others. It could be your attitude or feelings for something in particular. The reason for hiding them could be because you do not feel that your views are supported within the group or that you want to keep the information as a way of manipulating the group or the situation. Keeping information in, consumes your energy.

The Unknown Field:

In the unknown field are things that neither you, nor anyone in the group, know about you. Some of the things in the unknown field can be exposed through feedback and will then hopefully lead to insights, increasing your arena and decreasing the unknown field. Certain things in the unknown field lie so deeply that you may never see them. It can, for example, be memories from early childhood. Things like these gather in the subconscious part of the brain and cannot be removed easily.

In certain situations, talents you did not know you had emerge from the unknown field. For example, if you take up a new sport or manage to paint a very good picture. The skill has been there all the time, developing throughout your life without you knowing.

I believe we carry many things with us in the unknown field which we never use. By learning to trust the unknown field, we develop an inner belief that we can create so much more than we are aware of. It is up to you as an individual to discover the inner potential that you carry.

In conclusion, you could say that the size of the different fields varies according to the degree of openness you choose to have and the group's ability to give and receive feedback. To develop and influence the size of the different fields, you need to ask the people around you for feedback.

PATIENCE AND REFLECTION

People accept feedback in different ways. Some recognise themselves in the feedback they are given and immediately make a change. As I mentioned earlier, there are also people who prefer to reflect a little longer than others over the feedback they receive. This must clearly be respected. These people must also get a chance to ask other friends or colleagues if they also experience that he or she has the negative or bad behaviour that you have highlighted in your feedback.

You should also bear in mind that not everyone wants what's best for you. Reflect on the feedback you receive. Is the person correct or does he just want to hurt you? Does he want to influence you positively or pull you down? What are the person's motives for such feedback? Feedback should always be given with good intent.

CHAPTER 15
ACRES OF DIAMONDS

Acres of diamonds is a story which has been told thousands of times throughout the world. What can we learn from it?

The story is about an Arabian man by the name of Al Hafed. He was the owner of a large farm with great green fields and pastures. He was a rich man who was happy with his life. One day he was visited by a Buddhist monk who sat down and told Al Hafed about how everything on earth was created; how coal was compressed to create the diamond. He was told the incredible advantages he would have in life if should he have a diamond mine – he would earn so much money that he could buy an entire country. He would be able to do whatever he wanted for his family. That night, Al Hafed lay in bed thinking himself poor.

The following day he was determined to go out in the search of diamonds. Al Hafed sought out the monk and asked him where he could find the diamonds. The response was to look for the white sand where the water flows between the mountains, that was where he would find the diamonds. Al Hafed sold his farm and went in search of this place. He looked everywhere, but could not find it. Eventually he had had enough, he went to a river and drowned himself.

The man who had bought the farm from Al Hafed one day discovered, by accident, something gleaming in the river which flowed through the land he had bought.

He picked up the shining stone but, not understanding what he had found, he brought it home and placed it on the mantelpiece. He thought it to be a very nice stone. A few days later he was visited by the monk who had given Al Hafed the tip to search for diamonds. The monk saw the stone and exclaimed: "Has Al Hafed returned? It is a diamond! It is a diamond!" "No," said the man, "I found the stone outside, on my farm".

Together they ran out, looking in the white sand by the river that ran through the man's land where he had found the stone. There they found more diamonds. It was discovered that the land the man had bought was full of diamonds – acres of diamonds. This later became the biggest diamond mine in the world.

What is the moral of this story? The man who sold the land in order to go out in the world to look for diamonds had not prepared, by learning what diamonds looked like in their natural form. Nor had he seen what he already had, but ran off hunting for something he already had but hadn't noticed.

YOUR ACRES OF DIAMONDS

What are your, as yet unexplored, acres of diamonds?

By learning to find your own acres of diamonds, new things can be created from which you can do incredible things. There are several well-known examples. Amongst them, the man who owned a petrol pump which people would use to fill up their cars. He thought it silly that people just stood there waiting, while their cars' tanks filled up. So he began selling sweets, drinks and fishing equipment to those that filled up their cars. His concept was successful and became what we now call service stations. He started digging in the ground he already owned and there he found his diamonds.

What do you currently do? Do you have your own business? Are you employed? Are you a student? Regardless, you can find your own acres of diamonds. You can liken this story to the old saying: "You reap what you sow". But with the addition that you must first prepare the land that you sow. If Al Hafed had prepared the land he was to sow, by learning more about diamonds and searched the land he already owned, he would have been able to identify masses of diamonds on his land from the start.

He would have been able to harvest far more wealth than what he went half way around the world looking for in vain, ending with him taking his own life.

Learn from this and start preparing the land that you stand on. Learn more about what you want to do for a living, this way you will begin to see the possibilities where you are today.

LEARNING TO SEE POSSIBILITIES

How do you learn to see possibilities?

To go back to the *prepare the land-sow-harvest* principle, it is a process we must all go through in order to see the possibilities around us. If we think about how we prepare the land for finding our acres of diamonds, a mental process is needed. We must start to see things outside of the frameworks put up by ourselves or others in our lives.

We started this book with the *prison of thought* and you learned how to see new possibilities and solutions when, at first glance, it seemed impossible to solve a task. To demonstrate how easy it is to think outside of the frameworks, I recommended the following exercise: Take an ordinary paper clip and hold it in front of you. Write down at least thirty new uses for this piece of metal. What can you use a clip for other than for fastening paper together? You might have to think for a while, but in time you will find that it is fun and exciting to do this type of exercise. Some people find it very hard, but keep going, your hard work will pay off.

When you have finished finding new uses for the clip, you can exchange the clip for your business, your hobby or whatever it is you want to find new possibilities for. Perhaps how you will find more spare time to spend with your family – or whatever it is that you want to do with your children when you have some spare time. To take the exercise a step further, you can work together with other people and carry out your planning at a meta-level. This means that, just as you did earlier, you sit separately and write down some new ideas concerning a topic, writing each idea on a piece of paper. When everyone has finished, you stick the pieces of paper on a wall in no particular order. The next step is to get together and remove the duplicates and categorise the notes into different areas, thus making it easier to take your ideas further in a later stage. When you have finished categorising, you write down what you have concluded and summarise it for the next meeting. It is from these new ideas that you can decide where you want to prioritise your energy.

The next step is to sow. *How* you sow, is of course dependent upon the situation. Here are some examples:

Imagine being in a restaurant, the waiter walks past, slips on the floor and spills hot coffee in your lap. You can either get angry with him or see the possibilities in this situation. You might not have a eureka moment immediately, but the situation will sow a seed.

By thinking about the situation with the hot coffee, you are watering the seed you have sowed. You have started to ask people who know about flooring, and realise that there is a possibility to make a floor that does not get slippery when coffee or food is spilled on it. What you are doing now, is continuing to water the seed growing inside you. As time goes on, your seed will continue to grow and, once you decide to develop and patent the new floor, you will reap your harvest. This is where you are rewarded for looking for possibilities in having coffee spilt and being burnt. Instead of a floor, you may invent a cream to be carried around in case of burns. It might work as an ordinary hand-cream which people carry with them anyway.

Possibility is all around us. In your line of work, there are possibilities waiting for you. You must learn to see these in order to be a part of them. If you don't, somebody else will.

CONCLUSION

Have you ever dreamt of winning a competition with millions of competitors? I know that you have already been in such a competition and that you won, otherwise I wouldn't have had the privilege of you reading my book right now. To have the possibility of influencing you to start thinking in new ways, to awaken new thoughts in you, is something that I am very grateful for. You are the one who won the competition where millions competed, and now you are here on earth with your family, friends and other people. There is no-one on earth like you. You are the only one on earth who looks like you, thinks like you and has the same experiences as you – you are unique!

Think of the song that Gabriella sings in the film *As it is in Heaven*: "Now is the time that life is mine, this is my time on earth": This is exactly how it is, your life is NOW. We have been given a limited period of time on earth to make an impression, to add something new to society and to help people in need. I hope you use your time carefully and make something good of it, since you will not get another chance. Now is the time that life is yours! Don't sit in the retirement home thinking back upon all the things you could have done. Do it now instead of having regrets in your old age.

Even if you do have regrets when you begin to age, bear in mind that Edison, Einstein and many more geniuses continued to be creative and successful even after turning eighty. Many people at that age have started their own companies and become incredibly successful. It is never too late. What stops you from taking the step to be something great or do something amazing? NOTHING! Nothing stops you, apart from your own thoughts. Your thoughts have an amazing power to create and destroy. If you learn to manage these thoughts, you will be able to do so much more in life. Learn to listen to your thoughts and learn to manage them. Start to question your own actions in order to reach a better insight into your inner processes. Learn to bring your talents to bare. Look for your acres of diamonds and become a creative force. Together, we can make our, and future generations', time on earth something wonderful and rewarding. I believe it is just like Belinda Carlisle once sang: "Heaven is a place on earth". If you have not yet discovered this, I hope this book has sown a seed that will help you to discover that you can take control over your life, making it just as wonderful as you would like it to be.

Finally, I hope you have embraced the messages I have chosen to describe in this book and tried them out in your own life. What I have written about has changed my entire way of looking at life and interactions with other people. I hope this can be the case for you too. I would like you to get in touch with me and tell me about the changes you have experienced after having read and practiced the ideas I have written about. Visit me at www.carl-johan.com and send a letter or read about the different lectures I offer and speak to me during one of these occasions and tell me what you got out of reading the book.

Remember to regularly repeat the chapters of the book you feel you need more practice in. Also remember that it is your subconscious that steers most of your thoughts and for your subconscious to learn something new, repetition is needed.

Can you see yourself reaching your goals and achieving great things in life? I believe you can succeed, do you? If you can see yourself as successful in whatever you do, then you will be. Now that you have finished reading this book, make a conscious decision to create a positive change in your life. Regardless of what the decision is about, you deserve this change. You deserve the best you can get out of life, never make do with less. Live life and create your future!

Carl-Johan Forssén Ehrlin

REFERENCES

Below are some suggestions for reading if you wish to learn more. From some of these texts I have used information, from some I have been inspired.

BOOKS

Ahrenfelt, Bo (1995). *Förändring som tillstånd : att leda förändrings- och utvecklingsarbete i företag och organisation*, Lund: Studentlitteratur

Bandler, Richard (2013). *The Ultimate Introduction to NLP*, Harper Collins Publishers

Bakka, J. F; Fivelsdal, E.; Lindkvist, L. (2006). *Organisationsteori – struktur, kultur och processer*, Stockholm: Liber

Brown, Les (2002). *Up Thoughts for Down Times: Encouraging Words for Getting Through Life*, Les Brown Enterprises

Hill, Napoleon (1992). *Think and Grow Rich*, USA: Random House

Kiyosaki, Robert (2002). *Rich Dad, Poor Dad: What Rich Teach Their Kids About Money – That the Poor and Middle Class Do Not*, London: Time Warner

Kiyosaki, Robert (2011). *Rich Dad's Cashflow Quadrant*, Plata Publishing

Luft, Joseph. and Ingham, Harry (1955). *The Johari Window, a Graphic Model of Interpersonal Awareness, Proceedings of the Western Training Laboratory in Group Development*, Los Angeles: UCLA

Pollak, Kay (2014). *Choosing Joy: A Book About Improving Your Life*, Stockholm: Hansson & Pollak

Pollak, Kay (1996). *No Chance Encounter: Meeting Yourself Through Others,* Findhorn Press Ltd.

Robbins, Tony (1991). *Awaken the Giant Within: How to Take Immediate Control of Your Mental, Emotional, Physical & Financial Destiny,* New York: Summit Books

AUDIO BOOKS

Brown, Les (2006). *Choosing Your Future!* Les Brown Enterprises

Nightingale, Earl (2007). *Lead the Field,* BN Publishing

Robbins, Tony (1996). *Personal Power,* Nightingale Conant Corp.

Robbins, Tony (1999). *Unleash the Power Within: Personal Coaching from Anthony Robbins that will Transform Your Life!,* Nightingale Conant Corp.

Storey, Tim (1995). *Personal Renovation,* Personal Renovation Ltd.

FILMS

Pollak, Kay, reg. (2004). *As It Is In Heaven,* GF Studios

www.ingramcontent.com/pod-product-compliance
Lightning Source LLC
Chambersburg PA
CBHW031520270326
41930CB00006B/446